Wisdom Energy
Basic Buddhist Teachings

Lama Yeshe & Zopa Rinpoche

Edited by Jonathan Landaw
with Alexander Berzin

Wisdom Publications · Boston

First published in 1976
Second printing 1982
Third printing 1984
Fourth printing 1992

Wisdom Publications
361 Newbury Street
Boston, Massachusetts 02115 USA

ISBN 0 86171 008 8

Illustration on page 72
by Andy Weber

Typeset in Plantin 11 on 13 point
by Setrite and printed and bound
by Eurasia Press, Singapore

Contents

Introduction to the First Edition

The lectures presented in this volume were originally given by Lama Thubten Yeshe and his closest disciple, Lama Thubten Zopa Rinpoche, during their tour of the United States in the summer of 1974. Both of these lamas derive from the Mahayana Buddhist traditions transmitted in Tibet, and over the past ten years have had continual contact with Western students interested in the study and practice of the buddha dharma. It is hoped that by publishing here a representative selection of the talks given by these lamas before Western audiences in a Western environment, those people interested in learning more about the possibilities of spiritual development will gain a clear idea of how the buddha dharma can be effective in their daily lives.

Lama Thubten Yeshe was born in Tibet in 1935 not far from Lhasa in the town of Tölung Dechen. Two hours away by horse was the Chi-me Lung Gompa, home for about 100 nuns of the Gelug tradition. It had been a few years since their learned abbess and guru had passed away when Nenung Pawo Rinpoche, a Kagyü lama widely famed for his psychic powers, came by their convent. They approached him and asked, "Where is our guru now?" He answered that in a nearby village there was a boy born at such and such a time, and if they investigated they would discover that he was their incarnated abbess. Following his advice they found the young Lama Yeshe to whom they brought many offerings and gave the name Thondrub Dorje.

Afterwards the nuns would often take the young boy back to their convent to attend the various ceremonies and other religious functions held there. During these visits—which would some-times last for days at a time—he often stayed in their shrine room and attended services with them. The nuns would also frequently visit him at his parents' home where he was taught the alphabet, grammar and reading by his uncle, Ngawang Norbu, a student geshe from Sera Monastery.

Even though the young boy loved his parents very much, he felt that their existence was full of suffering and did not want to live as they did. From a very early age he expressed the desire to lead a religious life. Whenever a monk would visit their home, he would beg to leave with him and join a monastery. Finally, when he was six years old, he received his parents' permission to join Sera Je, a college at one of the three great Gelug monastic centres located in the vicinity of Lhasa. He was taken there by his uncle, who promised the young boy's mother that he would take good care of him. The nuns offered him robes and the other necessities of life he required at Sera, while the uncle supervised him strictly and made him study very hard.

He stayed at Sera until he was twenty-five years old. There he received spiritual instruction based on the educational traditions brought from India to Tibet over a thousand years ago. From Kyabje Trijang Rinpoche, the Junior Tutor of His Holiness the Dalai Lama, he received teachings on the *Lam-rim* graded course to enlightenment which outlines the entire sutra path to buddha-hood. In addition he received many tantric initiations and dis-courses from both the Junior Tutor and the Senior Tutor, Kyabje Ling Rinpoche, as well as from Drag-ri Dorje-chang Rinpoche, Song Rinpoche, Lhatzün Dorje-chang Rinpoche and many other great gurus and meditation masters.

Such tantric teachings as Lama Yeshe received provide a powerful and speedy path to the attainment of a fully awakened and purified mind, aspects of which are represented by a wide variety of tantric deities. Some of the meditational deities into whose practice Lama Yeshe was initiated were Heruka Chakrasamvara, Vajrabhairava and Guhyasamaja, three major deities of highest yoga tantra, to name but a few. In addition, he studied the famous six yogas of Naropa, following a commentary based on the personal experiences of Je Tsongkhapa.

Among the other teachers who guided his spiritual development were Geshe Thubten Wangchug Rinpoche, Geshe Lhundrub Sopa Rinpoche, Geshe Rabten and Geshe Ngawang Gedun. At the age of eight he was ordained as a novice monk by the venerable Purchog Jampa Rinpoche. During all this training one of Lama Yeshe's recurring prayers was to be able some day to bring the peaceful benefits of spiritual practice to those beings ignorant of the dharma.

This phase of his education came to an end in 1959. As Lama Yeshe himself has said, "In that year the Chinese kindly told us that it was time to leave Tibet and meet the outside world." Escaping through Bhutan, he eventually reached Northeast India where he met up with many other Tibetan refugees. At the Tibetan settlement camp of Buxaduar he continued his studies from where they had been interrupted. While in Tibet he had already received instruction in prajnaparamita (the perfection of wisdom), Madhyamika philosophy (the middle way) and logic. In India his education proceeded with courses in the vinaya rules of discipline and the abhidharma system of metaphysics. In addition, the great bodhisattva Tenzin Gyaltsen, the Kunu Lama, gave him teachings on Shantideva's *Bodhisattvacaryavatara (Guide to the Bodhisattva's Way of Life)* and Atisha's *Bodhipathapradipa (Lamp of the Path to Enlightenment)*. He also attended additional tantric initiations and discourses and, at the age of twenty-eight, received full monk's ordination from Kyabje Ling Rinpoche.

One of Lama Yeshe's gurus in both Tibet and Buxaduar was Geshe Rabten, a highly learned practitioner famous for his single-minded concentration and powers of logic. This compassionate guru had a disciple named Thubten Zopa Rinpoche and, at Geshe Rabten's suggestion, Zopa Rinpoche began to receive additional instruction from Lama Yeshe. Zopa Rinpoche was a young boy at the time and the servant caring for him wanted very much to entrust him permanently to Lama Yeshe. Upon consultation with Kyabje Trijang Rinpoche, this arrangement was decided upon and they have been together ever since.

Lama Thubten Zopa Rinpoche was born in 1946 in the village of Thami in the Solo Khumbu region of Nepal near Mount Everest. From the house where he was born he could look up the mountain side and see Lawudo, where the cave of the late Lawudo Lama was situated. While his predecessor had belonged to the Sakya tradition of Tibetan Buddhism, the Lawudo Lama himself had been a great master of the complete tantric teachings of the Nyingma tradition. For the last twenty years of his life he had lived in his cave, attended by his wife and two children, and had spent all his time either meditating or giving teachings and spiritual advice to the people of the Solo Khumbu and neighbouring regions. His energy on behalf of all beings was inexhaustible and it is said that in his later years he passed completely beyond the need for sleep.

From the time he was able to crawl, Zopa Rinpoche would spend much of his time trying to climb the steep path leading to the cave of this deceased lama. Time and again his family would have to retrieve him forcefully from the precarious route he was intent on travelling and make him return reluctantly to his home. Finally, when he was old enough to speak, he declared that the cave was his and that he was the incarnation of the Lawudo Lama. He further insisted that his only desire was to lead a life of meditation. When he was four or five years old, his claim to be an incarnate lama was subjected to public examination by Ngawang Samden, a Nyingma master meditator who lived nearby. When the young boy was repeatedly able to identify possessions belonging to the Lawudo Lama and pass other rigorous tests, he was formally declared to be the rightful incarnation and received the full investiture of the Nyingma tradition. Later he was to receive the tantric initiations of this tradition from the head lama of the

Thami Gompa, known affectionately as Gaga (or Grandfather) Lama.

Young Zopa Rinpoche began his education at Solo Khumbu in the traditional Tibetan manner, with the alphabet. One of the first books he read was the biography of Milarepa, the famous eleventh century poet and meditator. This work sparked in him a great desire to become like Milarepa and study under such a highly realized lama as Marpa, Milarepa's root guru. He also heard of the Mindrol Ling Monastery in Tibet, the famous centre preserving and transmitting all the Nyingma teachings and initiations, and wanted very much to go there to pursue his spiritual training.

While still a young boy, Zopa Rinpoche was taken on his uncle's back for a pilgrimage to Tibet. When he arrived north of Sikkim at the Dung-kar Monastery of Domo Geshe Rinpoche, he startled his uncle by declaring that he had no intention of returning home with him. Rather, he wanted to stay at this monastery and devote his life to studying and practising the dharma. The uncle was very upset because the young rinpoche was his responsibility, but when the commissioner of the area decided that the child's wishes should be honoured, there was nothing left for him to do but return to Nepal empty-handed.

The monks at Dung-kar had no reason to believe that this young boy from a remote region of Nepal was an incarnate lama, but upon consultation with their guardian dharma protector, his claim was confirmed. From that time onwards his diet was kept free of those foods considered unclean. His education would have continued at Sera Je in Lhasa, but these plans were also interrupted in 1959. Eventually he found his way to Buxaduar where he first became the disciple of Geshe Rabten and then of Lama Yeshe as described above.

Lama Yeshe and Zopa Rinpoche's contact with Westerners began in 1965 while they were visiting the Ghoom Monastery in Darjeeling. One day a monk came to their room and said that a friend had come looking for them. It was an American woman, Zina Rachevsky, who had actually come in search of Domo Geshe

Rinpoche, but because Zopa Rinpoche had been known as Domo Rinpoche ever since his stay at Dung-kar, she mistakenly believed him to be the lama she had in mind. From this unusual first meeting a strong friendship grew, and the lamas spent nearly a year teaching at her home before Zina had to leave Darjeeling for Ceylon. She then wrote many letters to His Holiness the Dalai Lama entreating him to permit the lamas to join her. When permission was granted she returned to India and the three of them visited the Dalai Lama in Dharamsala. There Zina was ordained as a novice nun. In 1967 the two lamas and their newly ordained disciple left India, not for Ceylon as originally planned, but for Nepal.

The three at first resided near the Boudhanath stupa several miles from Kathmandu. After a few years, however, they were able to purchase land at the top of a nearby hill called Kopan. There they founded the Nepal Mahayana Gompa Centre in 1969. The main building was constructed in 1971-2, funded almost exclusively by the lamas' increasing number of Western disciples. When the first meditation course was given there in 1971, it was attended by about twenty students. By the time of the seventh course, held in the autumn of 1974, interest was so great that attendance had to be restricted to 200 meditators, the limit of the local facilities.

In December of 1973 Kopan became the home of the International Mahayana Institute, an organization composed of Western monks and nuns. This fledgling sangha, which at present numbers nearly thirty disciples, follows a schedule of work, study and meditational retreat designed to help them fully devote their lives to the dharma. They also publish teachings and translations prepared by the lamas and organize group and individual retreat facilities for interested meditators from all religious denominations.

Kopan is not the only site where the lamas have tried to provide a conducive atmosphere for actualizing the dharma. In 1972 they purchased land in Dharamsala, the North Indian hill station that for many years has been the headquarters of His Holiness the Dalai Lama, and since 1971 the site of the Library of Tibetan

Works and Archives. In a house formerly belonging to Kyabje Trijang Rinpoche, they established Tushita Retreat Centre. Here many serious students from the Kopan meditation courses, the Dharamsala Library classes and other centres have come to use the ever-expanding retreat facilities to advance their spiritual practice.

Nor are Westerners the only ones who have benefited from the lamas' compassion, concern and energy. Lama Thubten Zopa Rinpoche's predecessor had been requested by the Tibetan and Sherpa people of Solo Khumbu to build a monastery near the site of his meditation cave. He declined, excusing himself because of old age, but promised to establish such a monastery for these people in his next life. When Lama Thubten Zopa Rinpoche returned to Nepal in 1967 he decided to honour this commitment made by the previous Lawudo Lama.

At that time he was advised by the late lama Lozang Tsültrim, the abbot of a nearby monastery, "not to have a small mind, but build the new monastery as large as possible." Donations by interested Westerners and the Tibetan and Sherpa people of the area enabled work to begin on this project in 1971. In the following year the Mount Everest Centre for Buddhist Studies at Lawudo was opened for residence. Attending this centre are the incarnations of several great lamas such as Lama Yeshe's guru, Geshe Ngawang Gedun of Sera. And soon the young incarnation of Lama Lozang Tsültrim himself will attend. At present there are fifty children receiving a closely supervised monastic education that includes not only traditional Buddhist studies, but classes in Nepali, English, Tibetan, mathematics and art as well. These monks are mostly Sherpas aged five to nineteen. It is hoped that eventually the Mount Everest Centre will be able to accommodate 200 students and provide for both their spiritual and physical well-being.

In establishing the Kopan Gompa near Kathmandu, the Tushita Retreat Centre in Dharamsala and the Mount Everest Centre at Lawudo, the lamas have been very interested in providing students with an inter-connected system of facilities to assist their spiritual practice. Thus when a group of disciples from

Australia and Mr. C. T. Shen of the New York-based Institute for the Advanced Study of World Religions invited the lamas to their countries in 1974, this was seen as a perfect opportunity to explore what more could be done to help spiritual seekers.

The visit to the United States took place in July and August of 1974. No prior plans or itinerary had been drawn up, but at Mr. Shen's suggestion the lamas, accompanied by an American nun disciple, Lobsang Yeshe Dolma (Maryjane Mathews), decided to travel around the country to see how the dharma was being taught in the West. First they visited Geshe Wangyal at the North American Lamaist Buddhist Monastery in Freewood Acres, New Jersey (now located in Washington, New Jersey) and saw many of their students living in the New York area. From there they went to the University of Wisconsin to visit Geshe Sopa, a great lama who had been one of Lama Yeshe's gurus at Sera Je. Then it was on to Nashville, Indiana where Mrs. Louie-Bob Wood, a former Kopan student, had been giving Bible-dharma classes to a large group of local citizens. There the lamas gave many lectures (Chapter One), interviewed over seventy people and established the Bodhicitta Center for Developing Human Potential.

At this point in their journey, Lama Zopa Rinpoche returned to Wisconsin for intensive study of Madhyamika philosophy with Geshe Sopa. Lama Yeshe travelled on to Boulder, Colorado at the invitation of Chögyam Trungpa Rinpoche, and there gave a talk (Chapter Two) at the Naropa Institute and held many personal interviews.

The next stop was San Francisco and Berkeley. In addition to giving public and private lectures (Chapter Three), Lama Yeshe visited Tarthang Tulku of the Nyingma Institute, the Kunga Lama of the Ewam Choden Center and the visiting head of the Sakya tradition, His Holiness the Sakya Trisin. Then it was on to Seattle for a meeting with Dezhung Rinpoche, founder of the Sakya Thegchen Choling, and more teachings and meetings with old and new students.

Both lamas then returned to New York where they spoke at St. Paul's Chapel at Columbia University (Chapter Five) and met Geshe Lobsang Tarchin and Mrs. Dorje Uthok. In nearby Fair

Lawn, New Jersey, Lama Zopa Rinpoche gave a week-end meditation course (Chapter Six) modelled on the month-long courses given at Kopan. This was mainly for past students who had studied in India and Nepal, and on the second day Lama Yeshe gave a concluding lecture on integrating the practice of dharma into everyday life (Chapter Seven).

The lamas then proceeded to Australia, where they founded the Chenrezig Institute in Eudlo, Queensland, and then on to New Zealand. Such visits to the West are continuing to allow past and future dharma students, while still in their native countries, to meet the living tradition of the buddha dharma.

This present book, a selection of the first American tour lectures, came about as the result of Lama Yeshe's desire to provide a Western audience with an easily accessible presentation of the basic Mahayana teachings. To this end the lectures were taped and later transcribed, then edited, rewritten and arranged in a manner suitable for publication. The final draft was then checked by the lamas to minimize any distortion that may have occurred. The indulgence of the reader and the compassion of the lamas are requested in excusing whatever errors or deficiencies still remain.

Anyone who has ever had the fortunate opportunity to listen to Lama Yeshe and Lama Zopa Rinpoche can attest to the power, humour and directness with which they communicate the meanings lying behind and beyond mere words. Unfortunately, it is not possible to reproduce their verbal style in a printed form that would be easily intelligible to anyone not already accustomed to hearing the lamas in person. An edited version such as this—which strives for a uniform clarity of expression while preserving a taste of the lamas' spontaneous response to their varying audiences—must inevitably lack much of the magical glow and forcefulness of the original presentation. If, however, the dharma wisdom of the the lamas reaches a wider audience through such a publication, then any sacrifice of style will have been worthwhile.

The organization of the tour, the taping and transcription of the lectures—which were given by the lamas in English—and the many other tasks involved in preparing this volume were undertaken voluntarily by many devoted students of the lamas. Grateful acknowledgment is paid to all these tireless workers with sincerest thanks for their invaluable contributions.

Finally, to Lama Thubten Yeshe and Lama Thubten Zopa Rinpoche go wishes for a long life. May they continue their good work of spreading the light of dharma to all those in need of spiritual guidance. As a result of these wishes may every being enjoy the fruit of mental and physical comfort and happiness, and may peace amongst all people be established throughout the length and breadth of this planet.

Jonathan Landaw
October, 1975

Supplementary Note to the Fourth Edition

The second edition of Wisdom Energy was published in 1982 with an additional chapter entitled "How Delusions Arise." This fourth edition contains further amendments and its list of suggested readings has been updated.

Since Wisdom Energy first appeared, the number of centres founded by students of Lama Yeshe and Lama Zopa has grown steadily until there are now 60 worldwide. And publishing ventures, which began with *Wisdom Energy* in 1976, have increased to the point that Wisdom Publications now has over 50 titles in print.

Of all the changes that have taken place, the most momentous have been those brought about by the passing of the beloved Lama Yeshe in 1984. Since that time Lama Zopa Rinpoche, showing great compassion and wisdom, has assumed spiritual directorship of the Foundation. Significantly, it was Lama Zopa who identified the Spanish child Osel Hita Torres as the reincarnation of Lama Yeshe, an identification confirmed by His Holiness the Dalai Lama in 1986. Lama Osel has now entered Sera Je Monastic University in South India to begin his formal studies in Buddhist philosophy and psychology. In addition, he is simultaneously being privately tutored in a normal Western curriculum. As His Holiness the Dalai Lama has said, "... he will be ready to benefit many beings ... Osel will be able to bring together two very important circumstances: to be a Westerner, but with the wisdom of the East."

Dedication

Wisdom Energy is dedicated to the long life of His Holiness the Dalai Lama and all other teachers showing true paths to happiness, liberation and enlightenment.

Part One
Entering the Spiritual Path

1 The Purpose of Meditation

I would like to say a few words in introduction about the practice of meditation. Many people throughout the world, in the West as well as the East, are very interested in meditating. They are attracted to this practice and express great interest in it. Yet, of all the many people who engage in meditation, only a few really understand its purpose.

Each of us here possesses a physical body made up of bones, flesh, blood and such things. At present we are not able to exert complete control over this body and as a result we always experience problems. There might be a rich man whose wealth is equal to that of the entire world yet despite his enormous fortune, if his mind is tied up in an uncontrolled body, he will live in continual suffering. Rich or poor, none of us escape this problem. Try as we may, we never seem to find an end to our difficulties. If we solve one, another immediately takes its place. The conflicts and suffering involved in maintaining our physical body are the same no matter where we may be. If we have the wisdom to penetrate deeply into the heart of this matter and check the actual way things are, we quickly perceive the universality of this unsatisfactory situation. It also becomes clear that if we did not have such an uncontrolled body, there would be no way for us to experience the sufferings related to it.

The main problem we all have is the suffering of not achieving our various desires. These include the obvious physical necessities of food and clothing as well as such enjoyable things as a good reputation, the sound of pleasant and comforting words and the like. Some forms of suffering, such as the hunger of an extremely impoverished person, are more obvious than others. But in one way or another, we all hunger uncontrollably for things we do not possess.

Take the example of someone who was fortunate enough to be born into a wealthy family. During his lifetime he may never experience material want. He can afford to buy anything that arouses his desire and is free to travel wherever he pleases, experiencing the various delights and excitement offered by different cultures. When he finally reaches the point where there is nothing left to possess, no place left to visit and no pleasure left to experience, he still suffers from an acute feeling of dissatisfaction. In such a restless, dissatisfied state of mind many people go insane, unable to cope with this intense and pervasive suffering.

Thus even when there is no lack of material comfort there is still suffering. In fact it often happens that possession of material wealth increases dissatisfaction, because it then becomes even more obvious that such possessions have no ability whatsoever to affect or cut through the root of suffering. There is still the continuity of dissatisfaction, confusion, worry and the rest. If an accumulation of external comforts really were able to cut through and eliminate suffering, then at some stage of physical well-being this continuity of suffering would be severed and all dissatisfaction would cease. But as long as our mind is tied up with an uncontrolled body, suffering continues.

For instance, in order to protect our feet from rough ground and sharp thorns, we wear shoes. Yet this does not really eliminate the problem. The shoes themselves often hurt. They can pinch our toes, produce sores and generally cause discomfort. This is not primarily the shoemaker's fault. If our feet were not so long, wide or sensitive in the first place, it would be possible to fashion totally comfortable shoes for them. Thus if we look deeply into the matter we see that the source of this discomfort is not external, but rather lies within our own physical and mental make-up.

This is merely one example of the suffering experienced because of our physical body. From the time we are born until the time we must die, we expend a tremendous amount of energy trying to protect this body of ours from suffering. In fact, most people spend *all* their time caring for their body in precisely this fruitless, self-defeating manner.

But the purpose of meditation is not merely to take care of the physical body. We should not think of using meditation in this way. It should have a higher, more valuable purpose. To use meditation as yet another external method to benefit our body is senseless. This would involve wasting a technique of true, ultimate value on a vain attempt to gain relief that is at best temporary. Meditation would then be like the aspirin we take to be rid of a headache. The pain may go away, but that does not mean we are cured. After some time it will return because the method of treatment was unrelated to the real cause of the difficulty and thus any relief gained will necessarily be short-lived. As temporary pleasure and alleviation of pain are available through many external means, there is no need to use either meditation or any other spiritual practice for such a purpose. We should not squander the power of meditation on such limited aims.

Meditation is primarily concerned with caring for the mind. Although our body and mind are intimately related and interconnected, they are quite different types of phenomena. Our body is an object we can see with our eyes, but not so the mind. The members of a particular family may share many similar physical traits, but each child will instinctively have a different personality, mental attitude, set of interests and the like. Though they attend the same schools, their intelligence and learning will differ not only from each other's but from their parents' and grandparents' as well. Such differences of mind cannot be adequately explained in physical terms.

It should also be noted that there are children who have accurate memories of previous lives. They can tell where they were born, how they lived and so forth, and can recognize people and objects from these previous lives. Such accounts are verifiable and provide intriguing evidence for any investigator prepared to study this matter with an unbiased mind.

In any event, the underlying reason for different mental aptitudes among members of the same family, and for certain children's memory of previous lifetimes, is the fact that mind is beginningless. Past lives do exist. While we cannot go into a subtle analysis here of what does and what does not provide the continuity between one life and the next, the important thing to keep in mind is this: just as our mind has continued from a past life into the present, so will it pass on from the present into the future. The circumstances of our present life result from actions, both mental and physical, performed in these previous lives. Similarly, our present actions will determine the circumstances of our future lives. Thus the responsibility lies in our own hands for shaping the remainder of this life and those to come. It is very important to recognize this if we are to find effective means for cutting through both mental and physical suffering permanently.

Each of us has been born as a human being. As such we have the potential to give meaning and purpose to our life. But to take full advantage of it, we must go beyond what the lower animals can do. By utilizing such a human rebirth properly and gaining control over our mind, we can sever the root of all suffering completely. Within the space of one or more lives we can escape from the compulsive cycle of death and rebirth. As it is, we have to be reborn again and again without any choice or control, experiencing all the sufferings of an uncontrolled physical body. But with the proper application this involuntary cycle can be broken. We can escape from all suffering and dissatisfaction permanently.

But to escape from the circle of death and rebirth ourselves is not enough. This is still not an appropriate way of using our human capabilities to the utmost. We are not the only ones who experience suffering and dissatisfaction; all other living beings share in the same predicament. And most other beings lack the wisdom—the dharma eye of wisdom—to find the correct path to the cessation of their suffering. All creatures on Earth, without exception, spend their whole life, day and night, searching for a way to overcome suffering and experience pleasure and happiness. But because their minds are clouded in ignorance, this search is in vain. Instead of leading to the intended goal, it brings them only further frustration and pain. They try to remove the cause of their suffering but instead only remove themselves further and further from nirvana, the true cessation of suffering.

All living beings suffer and desire release in the same way we do. If we realize this, it becomes apparent that it is selfish to work solely towards our own liberation, our own experience of nirvana. Rather we must strive to free all others as well. But in order to enlighten others as to the correct paths leading to a true cessation of suffering, we ourselves must first become fully enlightened beings. In other words, we must achieve buddhahood in order to help liberate others.

The situation can be explained like this. Suppose we want to bring a friend to a beautiful park so that she can enjoy it. If we are blind there is no way for us to lead her there no matter how much we may so desire. It is necessary for us to have good vision and to be well-acquainted with the road leading to the park before we can even think of bringing her there. In the same way, we must have a complete experience of full enlightenment before we can discern the best paths whereby all beings, with their varying mental aptitudes and temperaments, can be led to their own liberation from suffering.

Thus when we talk about the true purpose of meditation we are talking about the attainment of enlightenment, an attainment that enables us to fulfil not only our own aims but also those of all others. This is the entire purpose of and the only reason for engaging in meditation. All the great yogis and meditational masters of the past have practised the dharma with just this purpose in mind. Likewise, when we meditate—and in Buddha's teachings there are literally hundreds of different meditations to choose from depending on our level of realization—we should do so with this same motivation.

Thus spiritual practices are very necessary. We are not compelled to meditate by some outside agent, by other people, or by God. Rather, just as we are responsible for our own suffering, so are we solely responsible for our own cure. We have created the situation in which we find ourselves, and it is up to us to create the circumstances for our release. Therefore, as suffering permeates our life, we have to do something in addition to our regular daily routine. This "something" is spiritual practice or, in other words, meditation. If we do not turn inwards and train our mind, but instead expend all our energy on arranging and rearranging the external aspects of our existence, then our suffering will continue. Our suffering has had no beginning, and if we do not adopt an effective spiritual practice, neither will it have an end.

Generally speaking, it is difficult to practise the dharma in an environment of great material abundance. This is because there are many distractions to interfere with our meditation. However, the actual root of these distractions is not in the environment itself. It is not in the machines of industry, our food, or anything like that. It is within our own mind. It has been a pleasant surprise for me during this, my first visit to the West, to see that along with material progress there is substantial interest here in dharma practice and in meditation of various types. Many people are sincerely searching for the higher meaning of human life, trying to transcend the everyday, animal concerns of their existence. In this respect I think it is very wise that people are trying to combine a spiritual with a practical way of life, one that provides deep mental as well as physical comfort. For such people life will certainly not be an empty promise.

Food prepared from many different ingredients can be truly delicious. In the same way, if we have a job or some such daily activity and also try to work as much as possible on perfecting a spiritual path and following the dharma, our life can become very rich. The benefits we experience by combining these two approaches to life are far-reaching.

There is a great difference between the mind, feelings and experiences of someone who adds an understanding of dharma to his or her daily life and one who does not. The former meets with far less confusion and experiences far less suffering when encountering difficulties in the material world. He has a controlled mind and a meaningful framework within which he can handle his problems skilfully. This will apply not only to his everyday experiences but especially to those encountered when he dies.

If we have never engaged in any spiritual practice, have never trained our mind through the discipline of meditation, then the experiences surrounding our death can be very frightening indeed. For the most advanced dharma practitioner, however, death is like a pleasant journey back home. It is almost like going to a beautiful park for a picnic. And even for someone who has not achieved the highest realizations afforded by meditation, death can be a comfortable, not horrible, experience. Such a person can face his death—something we must all eventually do—with his mind at ease. He is not overwhelmed by fear or worry about what he will experience, or about the loved ones, possessions or body he will leave behind. In this life we have already experienced birth and are now in the process of growing old. The one thing we all have left to look forward to is our death. Thus if our spiritual practice can help us face the inevitable with peace of mind, then our meditations have been very useful, although there are much higher purposes to which our practices can be put.

To summarize, it is not the external appearance of our meditation that is important. Whether we sit with our arms folded this way and our legs crossed that way is of little consequence. But it is extremely important to check and see if whatever meditation we do is an actual remedy for our suffering. Does it effectively eliminate the delusions obscuring our mind? Does it combat our ignorance, hatred and greed? If it does reduce these negativities of mind, then it is a perfect meditation, truly practical and greatly worthwhile. If on the other hand it merely serves to generate and increase our negativities, such as pride, then it is only another cause of suffering. In such a case, even though we may say we are meditating, we are not actually following a spiritual path or practising dharma at all.

Dharma is a guide away from suffering, away from problems. If our practice does not guide us in this direction then something is wrong and we must investigate what it might be. In fact, the fundamental practice of all true yogis is to discover which of their actions bring suffering and which happiness. They then work to avoid the former and follow the latter as much as possible. This is the essential practice of dharma.

One final word. All of us who are beginning our practice of dharma, starting to meditate and gain control of our mind need to rely on proper sources of information. We should read books of sound authority and, when doubts arise, we should consult teachers who have mastered their study and practice. This is very important. If we are guided by books written without a proper understanding, there is the great danger that our life will be spent following an incorrect path. Even more important is choosing the correct teacher, guru or lama. He or she must have correct realizations and must actually live the practice of the dharma.

Our practice of meditation, of mental cultivation, should not be passive. We shall not be able to break the bonds of suffering by blindly accepting what someone, even a great master, tells us to do. Rather we should use our innate intelligence to check and see if a suggested course of action is effective. If we have good reason to believe that a teaching is valid and will be helpful, then by all means we should follow it. As with medicine, once we have found some that can reasonably be expected to cure us, we should take it. Otherwise, if we swallow anything that happens to come into our hands, we run the great risk of aggravating rather than curing our illness.

This is my final suggestion for those beginners who have an interest in studying dharma and meditating. Spiritual pursuits can be very worthwhile. Yet even if you cannot practise dharma, a mere understanding of it can enrich your life and give it meaning. I think that is all. Thank you very much.

2 Approaching the Study of Dharma

I am very happy to meet Trungpa Rinpoche and everyone here. Rinpoche has told me that all of you consider the search along the path to freedom, or inner liberation, to be very important. I am very pleased to hear that. Actually, I didn't plan to speak to you today. I only came to the Naropa Institute as a tourist and you are already familiar with the kind of things a tourist can tell you!

Somehow, everyone here has been very fortunate. You have come into contact with the wisdom-knowledge of the dharma and have also had the precious opportunity to be able to put this wisdom into practice. Most poeple do not fully appreciate the complex causes and the rarity of such intimate contact with the dharma. They feel that they meet ideas and people by mere chance. But this is not the case at all. Nothing ever happens without a reason or without prior causes. Therefore you should not take your acquaintance with the dharma for granted. Because it did not come about casually or easily, try your best to take full advantage of it.

There can also be misunderstandings about how results arise

from contact with the dharma. Some think, "I have received a teaching today, but I'll probably have to wait at least a year for any realization of it." They are searching for enlightenment and despair that there is an interminably long distance to go. How typical it is of modern people not to see what is right before their eyes! When you come into contact with the dharma, if you are wise enough to listen to it open-mindedly with full awareness of its implications, you will see an immediate reaction in yourself. You will come to know something new and more profound about yourself and the world, and thus the very quality of your thoughts will be affected. If you digest a teaching in the morning, some effect like this should be obvious by the afternoon. There is no need to feel that realizations come only in the distant future.

You who have been fortunate enough to meet dharma wisdom-knowledge through your precious Rinpoche should not be lazy in your practice. If you collect teachings without using them, they will only be a further problem for you. Since the teachings can be given in an intelligent and logical manner, it is easy to feel that the knowledge to be gained from them is merely intellectual. You become fascinated by the intricacy and thoroughness of Buddhist philosophy and its technical vocabulary and eagerly grasp at the words of particular dharma explanations. Such intellectualization without actualization is only a source of mental conflict.

It is easy to have this mistaken approach to dharma. During so much of your education the primary concern has been the trans-mission and learning of words. But in a dharma centre like the Naropa Institute, mere words themselves are of little importance. They are but signposts to a more profound wisdom. What is central to your education here is your own inner experience of dharma. You must experiment with the teachings you receive and see for yourself whether or not the dharma is beneficial for your mind. If you do this conscientiously and open-mindedly, libera-tion is easy. It all depends on how aware you are. The key to making the methods of dharma effective is always trying to see how the teachings fit in with your day-to-day life.

If you become caught in the trap of sterile intellectualization, the philosophy you learn will only lead to conflicting feelings and emotions. Thus, instead of achieving the desired goal of mental health, you will fall prey to mental disease. This is not the fault of the philosophy itself. Nor does it mean that there is something wrong with clear, intelligent thinking, for this is quite different from dry intellectualization. The source of the problem is a grasping attitude towards dharma knowledge. If you are sincerely trying to actualize the teachings within your mind by experimenting internally with all you learn, then philosophy and doctrine can be very useful. The more you learn the more you benefit. There are no complications. However, if you devour the teachings greedily without stopping to digest them, you will only experience the suffering of mental indigestion. For example, you may become proud of your hoard of undigested information and defensively say that your conceptualizations are better than someone else's. This leads to nothing but trouble for yourself and others.

Why is it that intellectual grasping is such a problem nowadays? It may have something to do with the present state of material development. People continue to hunger for something new but are dissatisfied with the wealth of goods that technology has provided for their consumption. Thus they turn to the realm of ideas for the stimulation they desire and are fascinated by the infinite scope of knowledge to be possessed. They feel there is no danger here of boredom because learning can go on without limit. Such an attitude towards the vast capabilities of the mind, however, has nothing to do with true intelligence. Rather it springs from superstition concerning the nature of reality. The extent of this intellectual grasping merely reflects the depth of this underlying superstition that an accumulation of facts can bring security, happiness or liberation.

Do not take what I am saying as criticism. The point I am trying to make is that you should check your own attitude carefully. Why are you studying Buddha's teachings and what do they mean to you in terms of your everyday life? You may think and say that you are following a spiritual path to enlightenment but, when it comes down to it, what are you actually doing? If you investigate closely maybe you can point to certain actions you perform. But if you check these carefully and find that they are quite trivial and play an insignificant part in your life, then perhaps you haven't digested the teachings you've received.

You are studying and practising Buddhism, but do you ever ask yourself what it really means to take refuge in the buddha, dharma and sangha? If you think about this for a while and try to come up with a clever intellectual answer—as if you are writing an examination paper—maybe nothing will come to your mind. You may then conclude that taking refuge doesn't mean anything at all. This would be a sad mistake. Yet even if you can spout forth a stream of words and definitions, if your answer doesn't come from your heart then taking refuge still doesn't mean anything to you. Thus taking an intellectual approach to this question clearly shows that you have not digested what it means to take refuge. You have already cut yourself off from any spiritual comfort or benefit that may be had from the triple gem.

If your study of the dharma has been open-minded and you have sincerely looked to it for answers to your everyday problems, then taking refuge will really mean something. Speaking from your own experience you will *know* the value of Buddha's achievement of an ominiscient mind. You will clearly see how enlightened compassion far surpasses ordinary attachment and desire in its ability to bring about your own and others' happiness. In this way the answer to the refuge question will come straight from your heart, not merely from your mouth.

When it is emphasized that knowledge must come from the heart, this does not mean that you should blindly accept something as true simply because you heard it from a lama. This is as serious a mistake as mere intellectualization. It is important to understand the teachings through self-awareness. You must investigate the truth of what you are told, not merely accept it because it is well-advertized by someone in exotic robes or take hold of it because you are intellectually greedy. There is no place in Buddhism for the vague dreaminess of a supermarket mentality.

If you have been studying for a long time and still experience familiar emotional problems, you may tend to blame this on your lama or guru. At such a time you should ask yourself if you have been doing anything more than acquiring intellectual knowledge. Has your behaviour changed at all? It may simply be the case that you have been polluting your mind. To avoid such pollution the dharma emphasizes that understanding must never be separated from action.

What you do in terms of your thoughts, words and deeds is much more important than the mere facts you collect from books or even from lamas, gurus, yogis or whomever. The responsibility for your own liberation and enlightenment lies with you, not with your lama. Your attainments will grow out of your own personality and abilities, not out of anyone else's. It is a mistake to plead pathetically, "O Lama, what can I do?" It is precisely what you do with what you have, your own potential, that determines the effectiveness of your spiritual practice.

In terms of the broad perspective of dharma you are responsible not only for your confusion and suffering but for your release as well. If the study of Buddhist philosophy brings conflicts to your mind it is because you have failed to see how such knowledge should be integrated into your thoughts and actions. However, if you understand how to digest what you learn, even a small bit of the teachings can become a delicacy for your mind. It is like chocolate or an incredibly delicious piece of cake. Ordinary knowledge is nothing compared to this. Such knowledge cannot even provide a coherent intellectual picture of reality, much less an intuitive, heartfelt one.

As I have said, if you can put what you learn into practice you need not wait a long time for results. The benefits come immediately. I am sure that those of you who have experienced completely integrated meditations have seen how all the ensuing problems of the day can be handled intuitively, almost effortlessly. This happens because even a brief meditation session can bring you deep peace, and such an experience is itself a realization, isn't it? When you are quiet inside, when you are the embodiment of inner peace, then you are really learning and it is easy to solve problems. Without such peace, learning only agitates your emotions. Your inner space is so full of the popcorn of your conflicting thoughts that there is no room for dharma cake.

Buddha's teachings are so simple and straightforward. If you find them complicated, it is only because you have made them so. You may think, "I have a Ph.D. and have amassed all this knowledge, yet I still can't figure out how to begin practising dharma." The remedy is to take a good look at your own mind. Try to observe your false mental conceptions and investigate the energy of your body, speech and mind to see if it is blocked or misdirected. In order to do this effectively you must have gained some control over your mind. It is for this reason that mental discipline, or mental rule, becomes so vital to your practice.

If you do not begin now to develop a mental rule or guide, you will have to spend countless lifetimes with an undisciplined mind. As has been true since beginningless time, the compulsive energy of ignorance will drive you to take repeated rebirths involuntarily. You will be completely open to adverse influences coming from within and without. In this context, being "open" has a negative connotation. However, with the correct application of mental discipline you can open up in a positive sense.

Mental discipline is not a neurotic constriction of your thoughts. It does not mean that you imprison yourself in un-natural and non-spontaneous conduct. Rather it means that you develop an acute awareness of *all* your actions. Slowly and gradually you untie the knots of your mistaken conceptions, thereby freeing yourself from the negative energy that has held you fast for so long. A complicated theoretical understanding is not necessary for this process to be effective. What is important is that you cease to act unconsciously, unaware of the consequences of your behaviour.

Some people think that having self-discipline prevents you from being open and natural. They think you should just relax and let everything flow freely. But to do so is not contradictory to being disciplined. In fact, you can only be truly open if you *are* disciplined. It is true that you must stop being self-conscious in order to be spontaneous, but it is likewise true that you should never be reckless and act without thinking. When you are well-disciplined with the wisdom of dharma knowledge, you are no longer under the compelling control of your delusions and ignorance. If you tried to act spontaneously without such mental rule, then instead of being open to the situations before you, you would be blinded by your own confusion. Therefore, to be natural and spontaneous, and not self-conscious, you must have the discipline that comes from self-awareness and wisdom.

People complain that it is difficult to keep a constant watch over the actions of their body, speech and mind. But this is difficult only because they are not aware of cause and effect. Your present behaviour exerts a direct influence on what you will experience in the future. Likewise, whatever happens to you now is the result of what you have done in the past. If you can realize this, you will come to appreciate that your present predicament is fundamentally your own responsibility and no one else's. You will see that it is basically your own decision as to whether you are happy or miserable. If you have the discipline of being kind, loving and open, you will be happy as a result. If you are mindlessly cruel, selfish and closed, you will experience only suffering. Discipline, then, is a difficult chore only as long as there is ignorance of cause and effect and therefore no motivation to be mindful. If you understand the intimate relationship between actions and their consequences for yourself and others, you will automatically be careful and conscientious. This is what it means to have self-awareness.

When you become more conscious of your actions, you develop more and more wisdom. Then you are really able to control cause and effect. In other words, you can exert a conscious influence on your karma. Thus with self-awareness you can be truly spontaneous and not at the mercy of your ignorance. In the mantra that is often used as an opening to discourses—*om muni muni mahamuniye svaha*—the profound meaning of the three repetitions of *muni* is control. The first *muni* indicates control over the three poisonous minds—ignorance, attachment and aversion—that bring misery into your life. The second is control over *all* delusion and karma, including even those virtuous actions that, while bringing worldly pleasure, still keep your mind unsubdued. With the generation of such control you attain complete liberation from cyclic existence. But you cannot develop such power or attain such blissful freedom with a snap of the fingers. It comes slowly, very slowly, developing within your consciousness and finally becoming perfect.

Mahamuniye, greatest control, indicates control over even the imprints of delusion and karma, as well as over the subtle dualistic mind. At this highest level of development, with the attainment of full enlightenment, you will be able to exert universal control and thereby benefit all beings. But you must begin slowly and proceed smoothly. Actualization does not come from jumping about. It is the result of steady application. If you begin gradually, you will be able to continue easily and comfortably. You will be aware at all times of what you are doing and how much progress you are making. If you jump ahead recklessly, you will probably only break your leg. Should a lama then come and talk to you about progressing further in your experience of the true dharma wisdom, you will just lie there crippled, unable to respond. Your inability to follow his teachings, therefore, is not his fault, but solely your own.

When you take refuge in the buddha, dharma and sangha, you commit yourself primarily to steadying your karma. This means that you should keep watch over the three doors of your body, speech and mind and maintain a balance in all your actions. The method for accomplishing this is meditation. If your commitment and method are clear, any study of philosophy and doctrine will be very helpful. The more you learn how to meditate and what to meditate on, the more effective will be your practice. Your life and spiritual practices will then take on a higher meaning by the force of your integrated effort.

The danger lies in missing the key to the dharma experience: integrated study and practice. If your learning proceeds with the force of tremendous ego energy, you will not absorb what you study and will consequently suffer the mental disease of intellectual pollution. For instance, you may have become very adept at manipulating words and concepts. If your study and practice are not integrated, this skill may become the source of false egotistic pride. Then even if Shakyamuni Buddha himself were to appear before you and explain the essential dharma, you would shrug him off thinking, "I already know that; you don't have to tell *me* about such things."

It is very difficult to change this distorted state of mind. Your mental energies can forge a powerful logic of scepticism that defensively holds onto cherished misconceptions with a vice-like grip. This cast-iron attitude not only makes it impossible for you to communicate with others, it completely destroys the essential value of your precious human form. Because you feel you know everything, you remain trapped in ignorance and squander this rare opportunity to tame your mind and escape from suffering.

Therefore, you must try as much as possible to put what you learn into practice. With great energy, integrate what you hear and read with what you do and think. That's the main thing I want to say. Be aware of your karma. "Karma," like so many Buddhist philosophical terms, is a Sanskrit word, but don't think that because the word is foreign the idea must be complicated. Every day you eat, drink, sleep, walk and communicate with others. All that energy is karma. To put it simply, whatever energy activates your body, speech and mind, that's karma. Every karmic action brings about a karmic reaction which in turn produces another reaction, and so on. At this point it is not necessary to complicate the subject. It is enough to state that happiness is the karmic result of actions done with a virtuous motivation and suffering is the result of non-virtuous actions. It would take days, weeks or even months to discuss karma fully. However, if the simpler teachings are not actualized first, the more detailed ones will be nothing but empty words, another intellectual game.

From your birth until now, everything you have said, thought and done has created the potential for future karmic consequences. There hasn't been a single moment when you have not begun such a chain of events. You may not believe in karma and cause and effect. Nevertheless, it is still there, like a watch constantly ticking. When you gain an appreciation of this ongoing process and become aware of how many unskilful actions you habitually perform, you can easily see how you continue to create problems for yourself.

Every minute you perform hundreds of karmic actions, yet you are hardly conscious of any of them. In the stillness of meditation, however, you can listen to your mind, the source of all this activity. You learn to be aware of your actions to a far greater extent than ever before. This self-awareness leads to self-control, enabling you to master your karma rather than have it master you.

In addition, Buddhism's great vehicle, the Mahayana, teaches explicit ways of transforming the most ordinary actions of daily life into an effective path to enlightenment. You can even harness negative energy so that it will yield positive results. This is possible because all such energy is an expression of mental attitudes that can be directed to virtuous or non-virtuous purposes at will. All that is required is alertness.

By understanding and working with your everyday energies, you can make great strides along the spiritual path. It isn't necessary that you cut yourself off from the rest of humanity by going into retreat. You can be learning all the time. Buddhism is a middle path that avoids all extremes. Therefore, if you are truly to integrate dharma practice into your daily life, you must strike a proper balance. Do not under- or over-estimate what you can reasonably accomplish, but try to work within available situations as much as possible.

If you integrate dharma into your daily life, you will always be filled with enthusiasm. Even when you are a hundred years old, your mind can be as exuberant and fresh as it was when you were fifteen. Otherwise, body and mind will grow old and feeble together. There will be no gain in wisdom-knowledge and you will live out the remainder of your life and die in fear and ignorance.

So please, as much as possible, try to be at peace with yourself. Try to be happy. There are many advantages to living in this country, so use them well. Remember that the true purpose of machines in such an industrialized society is to save time. If you can organize yourself wisely, you will find that there is plenty of time to meditate. Then, when you start to be aware of karmic actions and their effects by keeping watch over your body, speech and mind, you will really be practising Buddhism. Otherwise, when you try to meditate you will merely be sitting without performing any useful function whatsoever.

Sitting itself is not practising. Growth and development are the true practice. When you grow, you really feel it. There is no need to wonder, "O Lama, am I learning or not? Am I making any progress?" Your actualizations are experienced only by yourself, not by your lama or anyone else. You are quite capable of judging your own progress.

I think that I have already talked too much, but I guess I did have to say something. Now there is nothing more that I need to tell you. Maybe our meeting together has generated some merit, some good karma. If so, let's not waste it. Instead, let us dedicate it for the welfare of all motherly sentient beings. Thank you so much.

I am very happy that in America there are so many beautiful people searching for the everlasting peaceful path to enlightenment. It is extremely fortunate that you share such a fruitful karmic connection with Trungpa Rinpoche. May his efforts and yours continue to bring happiness and peace to all. Thank you so much.

3 Searching for the Causes of Unhappiness

An understanding of the true nature or reality of inner phenomena has the power to cut through unclear and foggy states of mind. Such wisdom is like a sword slicing through delusion. This diamond-hard blade is capable of destroying negativities completely. With the wisdom gained from deep understanding, your mind automatically attains a state of clear tranquillity and a truly peaceful inner environment is established. For this reason, the buddha dharma does not emphasize blind acceptance of doctrinal statements. Your own personal investigation and inner experience of the truth of the teachings are much more important than an unquestioning belief in dogma. Gaining such wisdom is the only effective way of training your mind and achieving your goals.

You will not make much progress along a religious path if your wisdom-knowledge is not functioning sharply. This is contradictory to what most people think about religion. For them religion is a set of rigid beliefs that are removed from or even opposed to reason. They are therefore assumed to be beyond questioning, logic, argument or scientific verification. Unfortunately, the deterioration into dogmatism of so much of religious thought strengthens this cynical viewpoint. However, I am not talking here about such degenerate forms of what might be called religion but which is in fact mere superstition. Rather I am concerned with inner disciplines capable of bestowing true peace on the minds of oneself and others.

It is a common mistake to think that a religious person is someone who is afraid of new and potentially challenging situations that might threaten his or her beliefs. As true religion is the very light of wisdom, why should a religious person ever be afraid of darkness? The nature of light cannot be affected by shadows. Similarly the clean, clear light of wisdom-knowledge cannot be disturbed by confused and foggy states of mind. Nor is the spirit of scientific investigation in any way contrary to true religion. After all, scientific experiments do not contradict the light of the sun and moon, so why should they be opposed to the light of inner wisdom?

The weak—those who lack the discriminating eye of wisdom —accept religious beliefs passively. Having no background in philosophic thought and ignorant of the reasons supporting their faith, they experience great uneasiness when someone questions their beliefs. Such people often live closely guarded lives, fearful of encountering someone or something that might shatter their insecure spiritual foundation. This attitude, however, is not the fault of religion but of their own limited understanding. True dharma leads in exactly the opposite direction. It enables one to integrate all the many diverse experiences of life into a meaningful and coherent whole, thereby banishing fear and insecurity completely.

Of course, the type of philosophy and logical thinking that underlies true religious belief is not exactly the same as that taught in schools. Mathematical logic, for instance, enables you to deal with a certain strictly defined external problem in a reasonable manner. The original problem is restricted in scope and the solution that is found completely satisfies it. Dharma logic, on the other hand, has a much higher and more all-encompassing goal. It deals with inner problems and looks for solutions to the most important questions in life: how to find happiness and avoid suffering for oneself and others. When you arrive at solutions using such dharma logic, you find that you have not merely answered one isolated problem, but have discovered the inter-relatedness of many inner processes previously thought to be unconnected. This type of reasoning, therefore, is very demanding, for you must continually check up and investigate the many hows and whys you uncover. But it is also ultimately more satisfying because it affects the very quality of your life.

How do you apply this inner dharma logic? Perhaps you feel unhappy and as a result the thought of hatred starts to arise within you. Rather than observing this process passively or being swept along by it involuntarily, you should investigate what is happening. Try to discover why you are unhappy and check to see if hatred is an appropriate response. In other words, ask yourself whether what you are about to express will improve your situation or not. Making such an analysis is not an act of neurotic self-preoccupation. Rather, it is a way to reveal the light of an answer to your problems.

Such questioning, then, is a process of causation in that it leads to a solution. It is the same as a scientist's trying experiment after experiment in order to come up with the best answer to his or her problem. While making inner experiments, you should ask yourself a series of questions in the same way. By doing this properly you will develop and mature spiritually, and as a result will overcome the uneasiness and dissatisfaction gnawing at your life. You will be able to analyze your growing hatred, for example, and discover not only its causes but an effective way to disperse and eventually eliminate it.

We often suffer from strong desire or craving for something. This follows from uncontrolled "happy" feelings experienced in relation to the object. When such feelings arise, you have to check up and see clearly what is happening. It is very important to investigate why these happy feelings produce the uneasiness of craving and desire. Similarly, when you are unhappy, try to discover why such a feeling leads automatically to hostility. Sometimes you feel neither happy nor unhappy about something. This neutral feeling often leads to mental fogginess, an ignorant state in which you do not wish to be bothered about considering the object at all. These three ways of responding to your experiences are not always gross and obvious but often so subtle as to be barely noticeable. As humans, we are under their influence at all times, even though we are usually unaware of it. Therefore, if you wish to train your mind, you must sharpen your wisdom and become more conscious of what is actually happening within.

When you look closely at the main characteristic of your feelings and see how they function, you discover something very interesting. If I can make a statement here, *all* psychological problems come from feelings. When a happy one arises, your uncontrolled mind is tossed here and there by it. When it is an unhappy feeling then of course your mind is uncontrolled and it is obvious that problems arise in its wake. Even neutral feelings, which are neither pleasurable nor painful, lead eventually to problems and suffering. You wish to ignore whatever aroused these in-between feelings and therefore you avoid exploring its reality. This reaction of closing yourself off from something is the very nature of ignorance and is totally contrary to the development of liberating wisdom-knowledge.

While it is true that feelings produce desire, hatred and other psychological problems, this is only half the story. These psychological states in turn arouse further disturbing feelings. It is a circle. Each is the cause of the other and they all spin endlessly in our consciousness occupying nearly all of our time and energy.

It is very worthwhile to look closely into the nature of your feelings and investigate what goes on in your consciousness, mind, psyche or whatever you wish to call it. This is so worthwhile, and who could ever deny it? Do religious doctrines teach a more effective approach for attaining true peace of mind? Are science and philosophy opposed to this method of investigation? Not at all. In fact, a background in philosophy, as stated before, only strengthens the realizations gained from such inner explorations. Without such solidity to your beliefs, you might feel you have an answer to a particular problem only to see it disappear when someone questions you about it. Psychological solutions should not be as flimsy as this.

Let us look deeper into the nature of feelings. Whether they are happy, unhappy or neutral, most feelings arise from wrong discriminations. Such discriminations are mistaken because they are based on false projections of the mind which keep you from perceiving the true nature of reality. This can refer to the reality of any phenomenon, outer or inner, animate or inanimate. Feelings do not only arise when one human reacts with another. They can occur in relation to anything. In most instances of conflict there is an object and your disturbed feelings about it are the subject. These may be thought of as distinct and separate from one another—as when one feels, *I* hate *that person*—but in fact your feeling has somehow created this object. By this I mean that the object of your feeling has nothing whatsoever to do with the reality of any external phenomenon. It is merely the painted projection of a falsely discriminating mind.

Therefore it is really quite simple to deal with potential sources of mental conflict. Merely remember that whatever arouses disturbing feelings within you is but the conception of the mistaken superstitious mind. Investigate the object in these terms and you will be able to gain a clearer view of what is happening without resorting to a very complicated line of reasoning. Just experiment with your life. Whenever you are perceiving, acting or feeling, check up immediately and see if you might be cheating yourself. Or, more accurately, see if your mind, projecting unreal discriminations onto the objects you perceive, might be cheating you by causing conflict and disturbances.

We always think that it is someone else who is causing our problems and robbing us of happiness. If we look carefully, however, there is no such enemy to be found. From beginningless time, throughout countless lives, and from the moment of our birth until now, we have been cheating ourselves. You may think, I never act that way; I'm a good person. But you will never gain absolute understanding if you look at things in such a simplistic way. Investigate your mental attitude towards things and discover how you impose your mistaken projections onto the people you meet and onto all other phenomena as well.

Most of the time we paint. We put our own limited interpretation on everything. You can discover this tendency even without resorting to an analysis of the ultimate nature of reality. Merely taking into account the relative, conventional appearance of things, ask yourself, "Who am I? What am I?" A certain definite picture of who it is you think you are will appear suddenly on the relative level of truth. Now subject this self-image to close scrutiny. "Is this who I really am? Do I in fact appear this way to everyone all the time?" When you do such an investigation honestly, this painted image will fade. As you see it disappear into unreality you will discover for yourself how distorted your perception of other phenomena must be as well. You will see that your painted sensory world is but the product of mistaken projections and that the feelings aroused by such a fictitious universe keep you shuttling back and forth between elation and despair. This circle of dissatisfaction, built on illusion, is samsara itself and your investigation will show you that it is fashioned within your own mind.

If you train yourself to look at things in this way, you will never think that your problems are the fault of society, your country, your father or mother. You will realize that the problem is *within* you. In order to prepare yourself for this task of self-analysis, you first need some instruction in how to think clearly. This will help you put in order the many diverse mental phenomena you will uncover. In addition, as certain truths are not immediately obvious, these must be shown to you beforehand by a trusted guide. It is in this sense that there is a doctrinal aspect to this process of self-analysis as well. But the true force of this investigation is your own unmistaken wisdom-energy which will give you powerful control over your life.

There is no danger involved in accepting this way of experimenting with your everyday experiences. There is nothing tricky or misleading about such a practical philosophy. You see that your mental problems arise from painted projections of an illusory world. Fooled by this illusion, you falsely discriminate certain feelings to be "good" an others to be "bad." But this illusory world is no one's world. Whose could it be? Investigate! My projection of "California" is no one else's projection. That is why buddhist philosophy says that in this respect all phenomena are created by your own mind. These words have a profound, essential meaning that cannot be discovered by the hypocritical, intellectually polluted mind. You must experiment and experience yourself the illusory nature of your projections. Only in this way will you be able to perceive the underlying reality.

Investigation is active. Meditation does not mean sitting in a corner and doing nothing. It is not like that at all. No matter what you are doing or what company you are in, you can always be checking, can't you? This is something that is always possible to do. It is a complete misunderstanding of Buddhist meditation to think it is designed for lazy people who do not want to work. "All those meditators do is sit around, eat, sleep and go to the toilet!" People with no understanding can think this if they wish, and even some meditators may feel this way. But a true meditator is someone who takes full responsibility for his or her growth and development. He or she should not be so afraid of everything that it becomes necessary to hide in a corner. Buddha never intended meditation to be anything like that. A small and imperfect understanding of dharma or religion may give rise to insecurity and a desire to withdraw from reality. But true meditation is an active, alert confrontation that pierces through illusion to the very heart of reality.

It is important to remember that feelings include more than mere physical sensations. They can be mental, emotional or sometimes even superstitious. All existing phenomena are the objects of one type of feeling or another. Most of the time, however, you are unaware of how you feel. That is why you must always look within and check yourself. By doing so you will slowly develop discriminating wisdom-knowledge. Such knowledge has the power to control unclear and involuted feelings and release you from their bondage.

Many times it is said, "Don't discriminate! Discrimination is the source of all problems." You must realize, however, that this word has two very different meanings. False discriminations arise when the painted illusory world of your projections is confused with reality and you compulsively think, "I like this," "I hate that," "He's right," "She's wrong," and so forth. These reactions have absolutely nothing to do with the nature of reality, and therefore such discriminations are totally deluded.

But there is a correct discrimination which is the very essence of wisdom-knowledge. It sees what things really are and helps your mind function in a clean and clear manner. Otherwise things would appear confused and jumbled together. Even on the mundane level it is very important to have this type of discriminating mind or you would not even be able to prepare your lunch. If you were to think, "I am free of all discriminations, so I'll just lump everything together in this pot," your meal would turn out to be a disaster, wouldn't it?

Thus, in order to look deeply into your mental attitudes and thereby discover what should be strengthened and what corrected, you of course need discrimination. Otherwise, who is there to check on you? When you are deeply engaged in meditation, for instance, one part of your mind should stay back and be mindful of the quality of your meditation. It must see if everything is proceeding correctly or not. "Is the energy flowing properly?" "Am I still holding onto the object of my meditation?" If you do not do this, your unchecked mind may wander off in ten thousand million directions. Some people think that deep contemplation means that the mind is no longer engaged in any discrimination whatsoever. But you must never do away with mindfulness. No matter what you are doing—examining a particular dharma point, trying to develop single-pointed concentration or practising deep penetrative insight—your meditation and your mindfulness of it should be simultaneous. It is very important and worthwhile to keep this watch alertly posted at the door of your mind.

Think for a moment how much energy goes into shopping in a supermarket. It seems so important and worthwhile to choose correctly that you become deeply involved in the glittering array of detergents and toothpaste before you. "Should I buy this? Maybe that one is better. Which is cheaper? That package is prettier."

So much energy! But while you are standing there in dazzled indecision, ask youself which really offers you more pleasure: these supermarket items or the wisdom-knowledge of your own mind. The pleasure afforded by the supermarket is quite limited. But the deep understanding gained through wisdom-knowledge is an everlasting, blissful enjoyment. This is true. Furthermore, no one can ever interfere with or disturb the happiness you obtain from such wisdom, because it exists within the potential of your own mind. All you have to do is train yourself properly and you will never be separated from this bliss.

You have such a precious, powerful opportunity to do something truly meaningful with your existence. But before you accept the practice of dharma, religion or any other form of mental culture, you must clearly decide what offers you the most in life. Can you really expect to find satisfacion in the maze of worldly desires, or must you search deeper for the source of true joy? If you never discriminate and make a clear decision in this matter, your acceptance of a path—religious or otherwise—will be merely superficial. There will be little spiritual growth, for it lacks a foundation deep within your own personality. Nothing clearly beneficial will arise in your mind because it will remain covered in fogginess and conflicting emotions. So please look inwards, decide what is truly best for you and discover the pure nature of your mind. Thank you so much.

4 How Delusions Arise

The purpose of meditation is to gain realizations leading to the cessation of delusion and superstition. This cessation depends, first of all, on recognizing the character or function of the deluded mind. In addition, it is necessary to understand the various factors causing such a deluded mind to arise. Regarding this, Je Tsong-khapa has explained six factors leading to the growth of delusion: (1) karmic imprints, (2) the object, (3) the influence of misleading companions, (4) following false teachings, (5) habit and (6) mistaken conceptualizations.

The fundamental cause of the deluded mind is the karmic imprint left on your conciousness by previous non-virtuous actions. Because of past actions done in ignorance and motivated by desire, hatred or any of the other delusions, various imprints—or seeds of karmic instinct—have been planted on your mind. When the conditions are right, these seeds ripen and the deluded mind rises again.

The object itself is the second factor encouraging this ripening. Most of the time when the object is there near you and the karmic imprint is there in your mind, bang!—delusion arises. A good example is when you go shopping. The object is there on the shelf. Through the sense perception of your eye you come into contact with it and before you are aware of what is happening, your mind sinks with attachment into the object. It can happen in a very sneaky way and be extremely difficult to separate your mind from this desired object. Your hand automatically moves to your pocket, finds some money and you buy even before you know what you are doing. It is so simple, isn't it? Thus when the deluded subject (mind) comes into relationship with the appropriate object, superstition explodes like an atomic bomb.

In the West it is incredible how everything is exaggerated so that the deluded mind is certain to pay attention to it. "Look at this; how fantastic it is!" This technique is used so extensively that even when we give a meditation course we have to advertize, "Come to our fantastic meditation course and learn all about your amazing mind!" Western culture seems a little too much for me.

Buddha gave a very simple name to all of this. He called the realm that we are living in the desire world. It is now easy to see clearly why he gave it this name. The desire world. Desire is here! The deluded mind coming into contact with desirable objects leads to superstition producing more and more delusion. It is for this reason that Milarepa stayed in a cave. He knew that once the deluded mind comes into contact with the object of desire, delusions arise uncontrollably. That is why he thought it better to avoid such contact until his mind was tamed.

The object causing the deluded mind to arise must have some relationship to the karmic imprint. That is why technically it is called a "related object." For example, you may have a particular imprint of attachment on your mind. This will be activated by an object having desirable qualities, but not by one having repulsive, hateful qualities. Thus there has to be the proper combination of both the imprint on the mind of the subject and the object's characteristic qualities. If there is no contact with an appropriate object, it is impossible for the subjective delusion to function.

The third factor mentioned by Lama Tsong-khapa is influences from the outside. Negative, misleading friends giving you deluded information are included here. These are the people you know who make you confused. Therefore whom you have for friends, whom you stay in close contact with, is very important. All around you people are drinking, for instance. If you have some kind of control, you may be able to remain uninfluenced by them for a week or so. But after a while you can no longer control yourself because the situation is too overpowering.

It is very difficult to maintain control in opposition to such influence. If you check up in your own life, I am sure that you will find many examples of this. Such influence is not limited to bad friends or good friends. In your life you have so many "teachers," people who feed you information that only adds to your delusions. Therefore it is very important to stay around those people who give you the right vibration, the wisdom vibration. This is much better than exposing yourself all the time to polluted, confused vibrations. But this does *not* mean that you give up completely on all misleading friends, hating them and having bad thoughts about them. No, this should not be your reaction. It is essential always to remain compassionate. Also remember that we are polluted already; our friends are not to blame for our delusions. Their influence just makes this pollution thicker and thicker.

The Western mind is very interesting. In some respects it is very sceptical, doubting everything. This can be a very good attitude, especially when surrounded by untruth. Yet in some respects the Western mind is totally the opposite of sceptical. If it sees something that has *one* good aspect, that has *one* interesting side to it, without hesitation it accepts the *whole* thing as good. This overly emotional attitude is very dangerous. Every philosophy, doctrine, and religion has at least one point which is good. Even the most evil person in the world—whoever that may be according to your interpretation—has something good about him or her. Therefore, the mind that runs uncontrollably to things that it finds interesting can easily grasp onto what is really not very good at all.

I do not know why, but it seems that the Western mind likes mixtures. Something that has many different flavours mixed together in it is seen as very interesting. Please check up and see if this observation is correct. In any event, such an attitude can cause problems in certain situations. For instance, you might be listening to someone expressing an idea which, in fact, is a total misconception. You think, "It does not matter if what he says is true or not, it is interesting. Let him tell me more." I think the Western mind is like that, having incredible curiosity and ready to listen to anything. But actually, each misconception, each piece of wrong information that you grasp at in this way thickens your deluded mind. That is why I said that this uncritical attitude can be dangerous.

All this relates to the fourth factor causing delusions to arise: following false teachings. This factor differs from the previous one, which concerns going together with those who are bad influences. The third factor relates in general to your life style, to your surroundings. This fourth factor, however, means believing that someone is a special teacher and therefore listening to and following all the wrong conceptions he or she teaches.

For example, at the time of Shakyamuni Buddha there lived a man who wanted liberation very badly, and so he went to see a certain guru. The guru told him to kill a thousand people and make a rosary out of their thumbs. "When you are finished, and have gained realizations, come back to me for more teachings." This man, known as Angulimala, actually believed this so-called guru, and collected 999 thumbs before he finally met Buddha and was persuaded to practise real dharma. His devotion had been blind, and led to nothing but suffering.

Teachings, of whatever quality, can be very interesting. But when people find things interesting it often just means that they crave information. The same thing can be seen in children. Before Western children go to sleep they like their mother or father to read them a story. That's true, isn't it? The stories are very interesting, but most of them are garbage. Children are very sensitive and have fantastic imaginations. They also believe in things very strongly, so that what they hear makes a deep imprint on their minds. Most parents are not fully aware of this and think, "It doesn't matter. As long as the kid likes this story and falls asleep, that's okay." There is no idea of what kind of effect it is having on the child's mind, what result it is producing. The important thing is that he falls asleep quickly so that you can be free, free to go to sleep yourself or whatever. Just as long he doesn't make any noise. But this is not right. It is not being kind to your children to give them such garbage information. It only makes their delusions and superstitions thicker and thicker.

Of course, if you have wisdom you can read any type of garbage information at all without being affected by it. You can be checking up on it without taking it all in greedily. That's okay. But when you are too interested, too attracted—"Yes, yes, tell me more!"—it leaves a very strong impression on your mind. There is a total lack of discriminating wisdom-knowledge, no clear idea of what is right and wrong. You take everything in with no judgement whatsoever.

The same is true about all types of information. So much comes in but generally there is no integration and no differentiation between what is useful and what is harmful. In fact, nearly every aspect of popular Western culture—books, magazines, movies, television and the like—is totally dedicated to producing more and more desire and superstition. There are exceptions to this, of course. Some movies, for instance, are different. But most of them show you what you like, what the superstitious mind wants to see. Anything to arouse your interest. The people who create these films, books and so forth have a practical understanding of psychology. They know exactly what arouses people's desires and superstitions and what will make them more confused than they already are.

In short, misconceptions and misinformation cause more delusion if the mind lacks discriminating wisdom-knowledge. You receive so much information from the television, for example, that you actually become excited. Sometimes you cannot take it any longer and have to leave the room! So whatever information there is that makes you become more confused should be avoided as much as possible.

The fifth factor increasing the strength of the delusions is habit.

It can work this way: at one time you had a certain experience with an object. When you meet a similar object you remember the first experience, and each time you repeat the action the strength of that memory increases, becoming more powerful and distorted in your imagination. Habit builds up certain associations so strongly that whenever a similar situation arises, your mind automatically runs towards delusion. Some people become so obsessed in this way with a deluded object that they cannot forget it. Why does this happen? Because the experience has been repeated over and over and over again, making the imprint of it thicker and thicker. The mind dwells in the recollection of this experience, adding to the delusion. A person cannot even sleep without a vision of that object appearing in his or her dreams. I am sure that everyone has had experience with this phenomenon. If a habit is repeated often enough and its imprint becomes strong enough, you can actually go mad.

Sometimes the object of delusion forcefully impresses itself on your imagination. For example, in the West when you are about to part from a girlfriend or boyfriend, you both plead, "Please don't forget me! Keep me in your memory. If you forget me, it means you don't love me anymore." That's why you are not free. You can see that you are not free because you have become obsessed in this way with one object.

The sixth factor also concerns things that appear interesting. When the memory of something comes, you make a certain type of judgement about it: "This thing is so good. It is fantastic. It has this quality, and that quality, and this and that . . . ." You exaggerate tremendously the worth of something until it does not resemble the original at all. It has become merely the product of your mistaken conceptualizations.

You have a boyfriend, for example, with whom you are obsessed. You find his every movement and gesture interesting. The way he walks, what he says, what he does — it all seems good to you. Even when he does something incredibly bad, for you it becomes a source of pleasure. You are concentrating so much on his attractive qualities that his negative aspects are totally obscured.

The mind works in such a way, however, that if one day he says something particularly unpleasant to you, your attitude begins to change. You think, "He's not nice at all." Your mind concentrates on this thought. "Not nice, not nice, not nice. . . ." Soon everything about him appears repulsive; there is nothing about him anymore that is pleasing to you. You can see this happen, can't you? It is incredible how the deluded mind works. First something appears completely positive and then it changes to its opposite. But I say that it is totally impossible for any object, any sentient being to be completely positive or completely negative. Everything has both positive and negative energy. It is only the obsessed mind that sees things in terms of black and white. There is a certain saying I heard in the West: "You hear what you want to hear." This is a very accurate psychological statement, a very good dharma point. It emphasizes the truth of what we have been discussing.

Seeing some kind of desirable object, then, always involves an overestimation. Its good aspects are emphasized so much that you lose all judgement about it. Simultaneously, you view that object as if it were somehow self-existent. You conceive of it as something permanent, existing self-sufficiently the way it appears to you. You fail to see that the way it appears is actually a function of your own projections. Instead, you think that these exaggerated qualities come from the object itself rather than being what you have put onto the object from your own side. You do not see what has happened. This deluded projection covering the object is much thicker than make-up. Impermanent things are viewed as permanent. Objects being in the nature of suffering are thought of as the causes of happiness. And although all things lack true, independent self-existence, they are conceived of as having such self-existence.

Je Tsong-khapa defined this process as holding onto something that has nothing to do with reality. It is completely unrelated to the way things actually exist. You grasp onto something, perceiving and believing it to exist in a certain way, and as a result your delusions grow. The deluded mind becomes more powerful. This brings us back to an earlier point: whatever exists—good news, bad news, heaven and hell, samsara or nirvana—is a manifestation of the mind. When the mind is covered with superstitions it creates suffering. Therefore, in order to gain release from this suffering it is important to understand both the characteristic nature of the deluded mind and the factors causing these superstitions to arise and increase. So check up and meditate on these six factors. It is so worthwhile. Your understanding can become so powerful that it makes your mind really straight. Otherwise there is no way to begin to rid yourself of delusions.

5 Understanding Suffering and Controlling the Mind

A lecture on dharma is supposed to benefit people by pointing out mistakes in their behaviour and by teaching them ways to solve the problems of life. This is why you came here to listen and why I came to speak. But a dharma lecture can be truly effective only if the teacher is a living example of what he or she preaches. Unfortunately I am totally unqualified in this respect. I eat, drink, eliminate waste and sleep, but I know nothing of dharma. Yet since I have studied under several highly realized beings, perhaps I can report their experiences. Whether this will be of any benefit to you or not is another matter.

It is very important to have a clear understanding of the purpose of dharma. Why are we meditating, following a spiritual path or leading a religious life? The purpose of these endeavours must differ somehow from that of our ordinary daily activities. If it does not, then there is no need to go to all the trouble involved.

The different world religions, philosophies, ethical systems and so forth are called by different names and have quite divergent teaching methods. But their essential purpose must be the same. If these systems of thought have any value at all, they must teach ways whereby the mental and physical suffering of all living beings can be alleviated. It is up to them to provide deep solutions to the universal problem of suffering because all externally applied methods have shown themselves to be ineffective in this regard.

Since life first started to evolve on this planet, a great deal of individual and group effort has been expended on improving our general living conditions. At present there are many organizations in almost all the countries of the world actively engaged in bettering the lot of mankind. Yet despite the stated goals and the untiring efforts of the many people involved in such societies, the world is no closer to peace now than it has ever been. In fact there are good reasons for believing that the times are degenerating. Why have the hopes inspired by material development remained so disappointingly unfulfilled?

A major difficulty has been that we tend to think of our problems as if they were external entities, things existing in some way outside and unrelated to ourselves. Consequently, the solutions we come up with are also external. Although such solutions may relieve a particular problem temporarily, another trouble always seems to crop up in its place. Therefore, while our efforts may bring about a change in symptoms, they seem to have little effect on the underlying problem itself.

Many endeavours sincerely designed to improve unwholesome situations have in fact only aggravated them. One example is the development of atomic energy. Whatever might have been the original hopes of the scientists and engineers responsible for its discovery and utilization, nuclear progress has certainly raised some grave, unforeseen dangers in terms of our conservation of natural resources, protection of the environment and the maintenance of world peace.

Why is it that our recurring dream of universal peace has not come true? Why do we continue to be deprived of the much sought-after cessation of suffering and confusion? Certainly there has been no lack of sincere humanitarians or theoretical doctrines designed to promote harmony and minimize discord. Yet there must be something that we either do not fully understand or do not properly use because, no matter how much we try to benefit ourselves and others, nothing ever seems to improve significantly. What is missing in great humanitarian projects as well as in our daily activities is an effective method for achieving our aims. A method can be effective only if it confronts the underlying cause of our problems. For this an inner, as opposed to a merely external, method is required.

Why does an effective method have to be internal as well as external? The reason is that the sufferings we are intent on eliminating are not merely external. If we believe that the source of all our problems lies solely in objects outside ourselves, we may try to eliminate, change or somehow counteract them. These efforts, however, are ultimately doomed to failure because the root of all suffering, without exception, lies within our own mind.

It can be demonstrated that external objects—that people, things and situations we encounter in our life—are not the primary source of our dissatisfaction and suffering. For instance, some travellers find a particular country so enjoyable that they want to spend a lot of time there. But others, even if they come from a similar background, may find the same country totally alien to their taste. The discomfort they experience while visiting there is a constant problem for them, but it cannot be blamed solely on the external situation. If it could, then no one at all would enjoy going to that country. Similarly, certain food appeals to some members of a particular family, but it often happens that others in that family will not even touch it. How can such contradictory properties exist within one and the same type of food?

An even more pertinent example may be seen in our relation-ships with other people. If someone is our friend we view him or her as being very kind and likeable. Whenever he appears, a warm feeling is generated within our heart. But the very appearance of this person to someone else may arouse completely opposite reactions. He is seen as so vicious and cruel that the mere sight of him cannot be tolerated. Thus the person who inspires love in us may generate nothing but hatred in someone else.

There is no need to compare our feelings with what someone else experiences to realize how varied such personal reactions can be. Think of our own reactions to someone we have met in the past. At first he was a stranger to us and we might have ignored him completely. But after a while he became a close friend. After much close contact we came to see him as truly beautiful and could hardly remember when he was not our closest companion. There was no doubt in our mind that he was kind, loving and the very embodiment of all virtues. We really believed this because our attachment to him was so strong.

But after a while circumstances changed. Maybe he said something we disagreed with or behaved in an annoying manner. Whatever the reason—and it might have been quite a trivial one —he now appears to be a completely different person. His speech is discordant, his manner offensive and even his face seems to wear a cruel expression. He is not at all the same person as before and the attachment we formerly felt towards him is now completely replaced by hatred. When we encounter him, anger and other manifestations of a negative mind arise. As a result we experience great suffering.

Thus it is easy to see that we suffer, not necessarily because of any change occurring in external objects, but because our own attitudes change. In different states of mind we see the same thing in varying ways. By and large, our entire life is filled with experiencing precisely such fluctuations in attitude.

These changes are often very rapid. Occasionally we are right in the middle of becoming angry with someone when all of a sudden a thought of his past kindness surfaces in our mind. We remember the time when he gave us some much-needed help or acted with unexpected selflessness. In a split second the radiance of such a memory can dispel the darkness of anger and we see him once more as our dearest friend. Such an experience—which must have happened to us all—should make us aware not only that our mind undergoes constant change, but also that if we could exert some control over this process we would be much happier.

If we are alert to what is going on in our mind, we can intercept negative thoughts before they cause us to be miserable. There are at least as many reasons to think positively about someone as there are to harbour hatred. If we have developed the necessary mental discipline and are sufficiently aware of what is happening inside us, there is no reason why we cannot choose to express only those thoughts that will bring happiness to ourselves and others. The whole world might rise against us, but if the ability to control our mind were well developed we could still view everyone as our friend rather than cower with fear and hatred.

If we could exert such conscious control over the mind, imagine the great peace we would experience! There would be no confusion and we would create no problems for ourselves or others. Such a deeply felt experience of well-being is a definite result of dharma practice. It can be gained by anyone with the perseverance to pursue an inner search along the spiritual path.

Solving problems by gaining control over our mind is not only the most effective way to deal with difficulties, but also the easiest and most harmless. We can gain true peace of mind without threatening the well-being of anyone. In this way we not only make ourselves happy but are in a position to bring others peace as well. Otherwise, if we persist in thinking that the root of our troubles is external to us, we would have to destroy every potential enemy in the world in order to gain security. Yet even if we were to employ such an unskilful method of dealing with our problems, we would still be left with an agitated mind. Since we have no inner method to clear up this mental confusion, we would continue to suffer even in the absence of external foes.

Thus if we are to deal effectively with our problems we must first discover and recognize the internal mental factors that are the cause of our suffering. Our method should be similar to the one a doctor uses when attempting to treat someone's illness. If he does not understand what is troubling his patient, he will not know how to cure him. Therefore first he gains as clear a recognition as possible of what is wrong with his patient, and then he prescribes treatment that will combat and neutralize the source of his disease. In exactly the same manner, if we are to solve our problems by following an inner spiritual method we must first gain a clear, undistorted picture of what is bothering us. Rather than succumb to the common tendency of hiding our sufferings from ourselves, we must face up to our problems. Only then shall we be able to remove each and every one of them.

Let us begin a brief discussion of the different aspects of suffering by considering the experience of the foetus and newborn. We do not usually think about the sufferings connected with conception and birth, but they are very real nonetheless. Because the mother's mind and that of the foetus are not the same, even she cannot fully appreciate the mental unrest of the being within her womb. But the embryo is in a situation that causes much mental and physical discomfort.

This small being feels trapped inside a narrow space which is too tight to allow much freedom. Sudden movements by the mother can cause much distress, as can foods that are either too hot, cold or spicy. He is confined close to foul-smelling wastes and can be disturbed by the unpredictable functioning of the mother's digestive and respiratory systems.

These sufferings might not be obvious enough for most of us to discern, but the traumatic experiences of birth itself are easily recognizable. When the time comes for the infant to be expelled from the womb, he is subjected to pressures far more severe than anything he has previously known. As he moves slowly through the birth canal, it feels as if he were being crushed between two rocks. This intense suffering does not cease once the actual birth is completed. His skin is so sensitive that even the warm air of the delivery room seems cold and harsh. The infant may be wrapped in a blanket made of the finest quality wool, but it is the same as if he were being scratched by thorns. In addition to these obvious physical sufferings, he often sees mentally created visions which are as terrifying as those sometimes viewed at the time of death.

Thus when we see a newborn baby, we should not think he or she is crying for no reason.

The vast majority of us have no recollection of the sufferings experienced at birth. This does not mean that we enjoyed our stay in the womb and experienced no discomfort while being born. Rather, we have forgotten all these experiences for the same reason we forget or are unconscious of so many things. Our ignorant mind creates so much inner and outer pollution that our perception of reality is obscured by a thick cloud of distortion. When we consider how quickly the memory of upleasant events even in our recent past slips from our mind, we should not be surprised that our earliest experiences are likewise shrouded.

No sooner are we finished being born than the sufferings of growing old begin. Our body goes through many unpleasant changes, and such things as childhood illnesses and the more serious afflictions of later life come as a matter of course. We do not actually need to contract a disease in order to experience the unpleasantness of sickness. The worry and fear of becoming ill also constitute very real suffering.

When and if we live long enough to experience the sufferings of old age itself, the changes we undergo are particularly distressing. Our strength, vision and hearing all fade and the activities we engaged in as children become impossible. As bad as these physical disabilities are, even worse is the mental anguish of realizing how decrepit and helpless we have become.

All the suffering experienced so far is only a prelude to what we shall experience at the time of our death. Every one of us has an innate fear of dying. When the actual moment of death approaches, this dread becomes enormous. Even though we do not wish to be separated from our body, possessions or loved ones, it is now clear that we must leave all these cherished objects behind. Moreover, we have no firm idea of what will happen to us or where our mind will go after death, and this ignorance plunges us into even greater torment.

Our deathbed may be surrounded by skilful physicians and concerned relatives, but there is no use in calling out to them.

When the time has come for our body and mind to separate, there is nothing they or anyone else can do to help. We all must die and have absolutely no choice in the matter. Throughout the years we have been pampering our body and giving it the best care we could. But at this time of ultimate crisis whatever bodily strength we have left is unable to help postpone our death for even a minute. Our inability to control what is happening to us is one of the greatest sufferings we have ever experienced. Thus we enter the unknown with our mind consumed by fear and worry.

All of us here have already gone through the sufferings of birth and we have also experienced some of those connected with growing older. There are still the sufferings of death awaiting us. Then this life will be over and it will have ended as it began—in misery.

In addition to birth, sickness, old age and death there are many other discomforts we experience throughout our life. For instance, we are always trying to gain possession of desirable objects. These may include such things as good-tasting food, fine clothing, attractive companions and the like. Being on the lookout for such objects but not being able to find them is a great suffering indeed. Even greater is finding such objects and then becoming dissatisfied with them. The suffering of dissatisfaction is one of the worst because it keeps us running from one thing to another in a vain attempt to quench our thirst for lasting pleasure. This pursuit takes up all our time, leaving no room in our life for following a spiritual path, meditating or practising dharma and thereby finding a way out of our predicament.

We not only suffer from being unable to find the things we like, but also from meeting with the things we dislike. All our contact with enemies, bad food, unpleasant situations and the like brings us much distress, mental as well as physical. This type of suffering causes us great confusion throughout our life.

Discontent and dissatisfaction prevent us from having any peace. No matter how much we possess, we desire still more. We work and scheme, planning new ways of acquiring objects as if we were going to live forever, or at least for several centuries. Think of what we do merely to take care of this body of ours! We spend a great portion of our life studying so that we shall be qualified for a job. We work at this job in order to make money and then worry about investing this money in order to earn even more. We cannot hope to live much more than fifty, sixty or seventy years and that time is all taken up with such feverish activity. But to what purpose?

We spend our life's energy in so many ways. We worry about keeping our body safe from hunger, cold, sickness, attack and finally death. Our life is a constant struggle to keep out of danger, and we virtually sell ourselves into slavery to accomplish this aim. We may hide this fact of life from ourselves, but deep inside we can see that all this activity is the very nature of suffering.

Although we work for many years to gain security, if the slightest circumstance in our life changes we quickly fall ill or experience some other misfortune. It is so difficult to find protection, yet so easy to be miserable. Even when we are fortunate enough to achieve those things that normally make this life more comfortable and rewarding, they are often only another source of pain. For example, we may save up enough money to take a vacation only to become involved in a terrible accident. Or we may go out to an expensive restaurant and come down with food poisoning. In such ways suffering comes without choice.

If we were to note all the different ways in which we suffer, the list would be infinite. What has been mentioned here is only a very brief account. However, every possible instance of suffering can be classified under one of three divisions: the suffering of suffering, of change and of extensiveness. These can be explained as follows.

Certain experiences obviously do nothing but make us miserable. There is nothing pleasant about sickness, worry, pain, fear or the like. Anything that plainly causes us unhappiness can be classified under the obvious suffering of suffering itself.

Other things, such as good food, fine clothing and so forth, do bring us a measure of happiness. But with deeper understanding we can see that these too should be classified as a form of suffering. This is because such pleasures are only temporary. They cannot and do not last. Take the example of eating good-tasting food. Most of us would consider this to be pure pleasure having no connection at all with suffering. But if this were the case—if eating good food were really a source of true happiness—then the more we eat the more we should experience pleasure. But this is not at all the way it is. If we continue to eat after we are full, our experience of pleasure will quickly turn into one of pain. It is for this reason that temporal pleasures are classified under the suffering of change.

If we have been sitting for a long while and become tired of this position, we may desire to stand up and take a walk. When we do so the sense of relief we feel is experienced as pleasure. But actually it is not real pleasure at all. We only classify it as such because the suffering we felt while sitting diminished after we stood up. And we actually believe this feeling to be pleasurable even though it will also change after a short while. When we eventually become tired of walking, what we once called pleasure will now be called pain. Thus no matter what we might think, there is nothing in our ordinary lives we can point to and call a real, true pleasure. All such experiences are impermanent and soon lead to suffering and dissatisfaction.

The third type of suffering, that of extensiveness, underlies the first two. It is the suffering of having the type of body and mind that is subject to and attracts pain in the same way a magnet attracts iron. For example, a stomach ache is an instance of the obvious suffering of suffering. The temporary relief or pleasure we experience after taking medicine is an instance of the suffering of change. But the very fact that our stomach functions in such a manner that it can and will become upset is an instance of the suffering of extensiveness.

Even animals can recognize the obvious suffering of suffering for what it is. Thus when we say that success in following a spiritual path largely depends on gaining an understanding of suffering, it is not this type that is meant. Rather, true insight into the nature of suffering is gained only when we realize that temporal pleasures are but another form of pain, and moreover that our mere possession of a contaminated body and mind is the source of all discomfort. When we have clearly recognized these two more profound types of suffering—especially the latter—we have then uncovered the truth of suffering.

Every instance of suffering can be traced to our having the kind of body and mind that is susceptible to pain. The mental and physical contaminations responsible for this condition can in turn be traced to those inner factors called delusions or afflictions. There are 84,000 such mental obscurations mentioned in the Buddhist psychological texts. All are based on the six main delusions: greed, pride, anger, debilitating doubt, distorted views and ignorance.

In the context of these root delusions, holding a distorted view means believing in things that are not true and disbelieving those that are true. Examples of the latter include denying the conventional existence of ourselves, all phenomena and of such things as the truth of suffering, its cessation, the mental continuum connecting one life with another and the law of cause and effect.

The first five root delusions, every mental affliction and all of suffering arise from our ignorance of the true way in which things exist. For this reason ignorance is called the "root of samsara." Samsara is the suffering state that every being creates for himself or herself. It is the cycle of involuntary and compulsive birth, death and rebirth, fraught with misery, in which we all revolve until we clear the obscurations from our mind. Jealousy, covetousness, pride and ill-will are but a few of the delusions arising from ignorance. These are some of the negativities obscuring the pure nature of the mind.

Why do we refer to these attitudes as negative? The reason is that actions done under the influence of karma and delusions cause us to suffer. Whoever acts with such a negative mind eventually must himself experience whatever unhappiness he has created. It is in this way that samsara, the circle of suffering or cyclic existence, is regenerated. Thus all actions producing such results and the delusions motivating such behaviour are called negativities.

If we want to gain true, lasting peace—the complete cessation of suffering—we must cleanse our mind of all these negativities. This is the only effective approach for dealing with our problems. For instance, if we are disturbed by the untidiness of a particular place, it is far better to clean the area then to destroy it. If we clean it up, we can enjoy it in comfort. Beautiful parks, for example, were not always in existence. The areas in which they were built might once have been very unattractive. But because the proper type of effort was expended in cleaning, decorating and beautifying them, these parks are now available for our enjoyment.

It is precisely in this way that we should work on our mind. If our thoughts cause us to be miserable, the solution is not to stop thinking. Rather we can use skilful inner methods and thereby clear away all the negativities deriving from our ignorance. If we work in this way we can gain true peace. This peace far surpasses ordinary temporary pleasures which, as shown before, are merely a more subtle form of suffering. This higher attainment results from the complete cessation of the very cause of suffering. When the root of suffering is cut, it is impossible for misery to arise again. We then experience the unmatchable pleasure of true, lasting peace.

We can now understand why there is no way to achieve lasting happiness unless we first root out our mental delusions. As long as our mind is cloaked in ignorance and other afflictions, nothing we do can bring us anything but the most fleeting experience of pleasure. This is because the negativities preventing us from gaining control over and subduing our mind are themselves instances of suffering. Whatever grows from such a state of mind must also be of the nature of suffering.

For example, suppose there is poisonous plant growing in our garden. If we want to be rid of this danger it is not sufficient to trim its leaves or cut back its branches. The only way we can be sure that this plant will not continue to send forth a poisonous stem, leaves and fruit is to uproot it completely. We must dig beneath the surface and destroy the root from which the poison originates. We should work on our own mind in the same way in order to free ourselves from our suffering state of existence. If we do not probe deeply enough, the most we can accomplish is the temporary lessening of a specific misery. If we wish to gain release from cyclic existence altogether, we must eliminate the causes of its suffering which are rooted in ignorance.

Ignorance is countered by wisdom. This is a deep understanding of the actual way in which all things exist. Usually we are quite deluded as to the actual state of things. As the discussion of suffering demonstrated, we are often fooled into believing a source of pain to be a source of pleasure. We do not recognize ignorance, the delusions or even our own suffering for what they are. We follow our ignorant impulses, obeying them as if they were our teacher and guide. The mind caught up in delusion is always projecting ignorant wishes onto reality, and in our blindness we follow these wishes as if they were reality itself.

Our practice of meditation, of dharma, can only be effective for solving our problems if it is aimed at combating this ignorance. A path is a religious one only insofar as it leads to the elimination of the very root of suffering. The specific form of ignorance that we must face and destroy with our wisdom is called "ego-grasping" or "I-consciousness." If we could check within ourselves at this very moment, it would be obvious that we are strongly under the influence of this I-consciousness. It is solely because we lack the proper wisdom of discriminating awareness that we do not realize to what extent our mind is under the influence of this root delusion.

What I-consciousness is can be explained as follows. No matter what we are doing—listening to this lecture for instance—we have a certain feeling about who and what we are, about the "I." This is the strong, instinctive feeling that this "I" is something independent, standing apart from everything else. We do not stop to think that it is in any way dependent upon body or mind or anything else. Instead, this "I" appears as something huge, concrete and independent. This feeling is always with us and we grasp at this conception with all our strength. As a consequence the thought "I am" becomes far more important than anything else. It is this tendency to turn the "I" into something it is not that constitutes the main ignorance keeping us trapped in suffering.

We can see the detrimental effects of such I-consciousness in our reactions to unkind words. Someone may point out our faults, blame, insult or criticize us. Upon hearing such words we immediately become depressed or upset. Our negativities arise instantly and we feel extremely uncomfortable. At the very same time, the thought "I" materializes as huge and strong as Mount Everest. From this monstrous "I" lodged in our chest many subsequent negativities arise, all of them producing suffering. In this way the ignorance of viewing ourself as a truly independent entity functions as the source of all problems.

We think of everything we perceive in the same fundamentally distorted manner. When we think of ourselves we do so with ego-grasping or I-consciousness. On the basis of such a wrong view, we are greatly attached to this "I." Because we view "my" body, "my" mind and "my" possessions as independent and self-existing, our grasp on them tightens and many negativities arise in relation to them. Similarly, because we view all phenomena as being independent and self-existing, we think that some are very beautiful and desirable and the strong feeling of wishing to possess them arises within us. Our dissatisfaction and insecurity lead us to grasp at these supposedly independently existing objects, but the comfort and happiness we desire from them never materialize. Thus our suffering grows instead of decreasing.

Not only attachment but anger, pride and all the other delusions and afflictions arise from this same fundamental ignorance. Because we think of ourselves, external objects and other people as being independent entities, we adopt aggressive, defensive or closed-minded attitudes towards everything. We become attached to those who increase our comfort and annoyed with those who interrupt it, while we ignore those who give us neither help nor hindrance. We classify everyone as "friend," "enemy" or "stranger" and think that these categories have real existence. In this way the great confusion of partisanship arises within our mind. Our attitudes are coloured by negativities and as a result the actions of our body, speech and mind are unskilful and non-virtuous. As explained before, these non-virtuous actions lead to undesirable karmic consequences which tie us tighter to the wheel of samsaric suffering. Thus it becomes clear once again that the root of all misery is our ignorance of the way in which things actually exist.

The value of any religious discipline, be it meditation or any other spiritual practice, depends upon its ability to help us cut through our basic ignorance and thereby free us from the suffering of the delusions. Whatever religion or philosophy we follow that provides a remedy for ignorance is to this extent a true and perfect religion, the real dharma. Throughout history there have been many great teachers demonstrating paths to the eradication of ignorance and the cessation of suffering. If our own practices are effective in cutting through this basic ignorance, then we can be certain that the teachings we follow are pure dharma no matter by what name they are known.

The Sanskrit word "dharma" has the meaning "to hold." In the the same way that we hold onto a pot to keep it from falling and breaking, true dharma practice holds us back from the dangers and wrong conceptions leading to suffering. Thus whatever we do, whether it be meditation or the way we conduct our daily life, if it acts as a remedy to our delusions then it is an essential dharma practice. Such a method does not depend on the traditional performance of certain rituals. Nor does it matter if the person following such practice is a Moslem or Jew, Christian or Hindu, Buddhist, agnostic or whatever. If what we do counteracts the delusions and cuts through the root of our suffering, then it is an essential spiritual practice worthy of the name dharma.

As there are different levels of delusion, there are different dharma practices designed to bring these delusions to an end. All the paths aiding in this endeavour are included within the subject of dharma. By applying these methods sincerely and systematically we can rid our mind of all its false conceptions, dualistic attitudes and negativities. In this way our mind can become fully enlightened. This achievement is possible because the delusions obscuring the mind are not one with it. The mind is only temporarily afflicted with the delusions in the same way that a used pot is only superficially covered with grime. Because the dirt is not the same as the pot, it can be cleaned away. Similarly, because the nature of the mind is clear, the temporary obscuration of the delusions can be removed.

Since the cessation of suffering and the attainment of full enlightenment are such precious achievements, it is worthwhile for us to devote a great deal of energy to following effective spiritual paths. Moreover, our practices and understanding are dependent upon hearing and investigating the truth of whatever teachings we receive. Thus study and reflection are also very important aspects of the path. If we study the inner dharma method as much as possible, integrating it with whatever external activities we are engaged in, then our life will have great meaning and be extremely beneficial to ourselves and others.

If we follow an integrated path we shall not have the gnawing feeling that we are wasting our life. In addition, when the time of our death approaches we shall not be overcome by fear and worry. Having developed a reliable inner method giving us control over our mental processes, we can face our death with equanimity, dignity and peace of mind. Knowing that we have lived our life in the best way we could, we shall be confident that peace and happiness will follow.

Everything described herein has been the experience of past and present meditators and followers of dharma. Many have become fully enlightened beings, achieving the final goal of complete purity of mind. In the same way that they have developed their mind to be without a single wrong conception or negative attitude, we can do likewise. Then, having reached this stage of development, we shall be able to benefit and help enlighten many others as well. We shall possess the selfless knowledge of how to guide others from their suffering in a manner best suited to their individual temperaments. There can be no higher purpose in life than this.

In summary, there can be a great difference in the ways we face our problems. If our mind is untamed we shall experience great suffering whenever we are thwarted. On the other hand, if we have gained some appreciation of what we can do with our mind and how we can integrate dharma practice into our life, we can experience happiness and peace of mind even in difficult circumstances. Although we may not develop the deepest insights of dharma, but have only a slight acquaintance with its practices, we can still experience great benefit in our daily life. Thus, as it is the concern of all living beings, even the tiniest insect, to attain true happiness and be free from suffering, it will be very worthwhile if we try to follow the dharma to the extent of our capabilities.

Thank you very much. Perhaps we have enough time to answer a few questions.

Question: How should we begin our practice?
Answer: The first important thing to do is study the dharma. If we do not have a firm basis of sound information, there will be no way for us to cleanse the mind. So first we have to study a correct method. We have to listen to correct explanations given to us by an experienced teacher. He or she must be someone whose life conforms to the practice taught. By following such a realized guru we proceed from studying the teachings to investigating them, seeing if they make sense in terms of our experiences. Then we must meditate on all we have learned, putting everything into practice in our daily life. In this way our wisdom will gradually develop.

Question: Is it possible that the methods of dharma taught in Buddhism, because they originated in an Eastern culture, might not be appropriate for Westerners?
Answer: As I mentioned before, there is no one type of action that constitutes the practice of dharma. Dharma is not something that has a definite form. Although people may meditate with legs crossed and eyes closed, these external postures themselves are not the essential dharma.

An action is considered to be a part of dharma practice solely on the criterion of its effect on the mind. If delusions are eradicated and sufferings diminished by what we do then this is dharma. Thus even if we spend most of our time working inside an office in a crowded city or doing menial labour and the like, we can still be practising dharma. The essential thing is that our delusions decrease in strength.

Any type of action can be transformed into a dharma practice if it is done with the proper motivation. If we keep in mind the importance of working to eliminate our ignorance so that we can more effectively help others overcome their suffering, then whatever we do is dharma. Buddhism, as one of the great world religions, teaches many methods for purifying our motivation. These are applicable to situations found in all societies, East and West. Therefore, if a Westerner has the wisdom to discriminate between the essential dharma and the cultural forms it has adopted, he or she can benefit greatly from everything learned.

Question: What is the relationship of tantric philosophy and practices to the dharma?
Answer: There is no way we can practise tantra if we do not have a foundation in the more fundamental dharma teachings. Tantra itself is a dharma practice and thus cannot be thought of outside the context of the whole dharma.

If we find a translation of tantric teachings somewhere and try to practise them without having an understanding of the essential dharma, there is no way for us to benefit. In fact, instead of these practices leading to a lessening of our delusions, they may only serve to increase our ignorance and mistaken conceptions.

The purpose of tantra, like that of all dharma, is to escape from suffering by peeling away our mental obscurations. Tantra is considered to be very profound because it is the most rapid path to the goal of full enlightenment. But the motivation for engaging in tantric practices has to be our desire to gain this enlightenment as soon as possible so we can benefit all motherly beings with maximum effectiveness. Only if we practise with this enlightened motive of bodhicitta will tantra prove beneficial.

Thus, since the purposes and the motivation of tantra are exactly the same as those in the dharma as a whole, these higher teachings are fully dependent upon the general teachings. If they are thought of as something separate, they will only lead to further problems.

Question: Do you advocate the use of drugs as a spiritual path?

Answer: No, I do not suggest that anyone seriously interested in practising dharma take drugs. However, I am not denying that for some people at initial stages of development the experience sometimes associated with drugs may be helpful. For instance, some people's minds are very closed. They do not believe in the existence of anything that does not appear starkly on the physical plane of existence. It might be helpful for such people to look at reality with a different vision from their usual limited one. This might open them up to further possibilities for developing their minds that they would not know of otherwise. But once this expansion has been experienced, continued use of drugs has the tendency to further engrain certain delusions and dependencies rather than help eliminate ignorance. But whether this experience is helpful or not depends solely on the person involved. Thus I would not advocate the use of drugs as a general method of entering the path.

Question: How important is it to have a teacher, a lama or guru while following a spiritual path?

Answer: Even when we want to do simple things such as travel from one country to another, we have to rely on the guidance of someone who has already travelled the path. If we want to speak a foreign language, we require the help of someone who is already familiar with it. It is the general pattern throughout our studies that we need the help of a teacher or guide to show us the way.

As true as this general rule is for most things, it is even more necessary when we are studying dharma. This is because the path outlined in the dharma is very unfamiliar to us. It involves radically different ways of regarding ourselves and all other phenomena. The main reason we are suffering is that we have become habituated to looking at reality through the distorting lenses of egotism and supposed independent self-existence. If we are to clear these stubborn delusions from our mind, we need the guidance of someone who has already achieved clarity of vision.

As it is vitally important for us to follow a correct spiritual path, the person we accept as our guide must be a perfect teacher. He or she must be a living exemplar of the dharma. At the very least his or her mind must be fully acquainted with the stages of the correct practice and he or she must possess faultless understanding. If we receive correct explanations from such a teacher and then study, investigate and meditate upon them properly we can achieve the desired results. If we rely on a teacher who does not have all the proper qualifications, however, there is always the danger that our practices will be mistaken and unsuccessful.

Question: How does one avoid becoming attached to spiritual practices?

Answer: Some people may desire to follow a spiritual path because they want to make an impression on someone else. They like the idea of being considered a holy or spiritual person. This is obviously a misuse of the dharma. But if we sincerely wish to achieve a true cessation of suffering because we desire peace for ourselves and all others, then such a desire is not a negativity. It is not at all similar to the type of attachment that causes problems for us. In fact, at the initial stages of the path such a desire is most beneficial and is not something to be avoided.

Negative attachments always bring us suffering. With a greedy motivation we do non-virtuous actions which cause harm to ourselves and others. But the desire, interest and energy to practise dharma are not examples of such greed. They are quite different. The motivation to practise dharma spurs us on to engage in practices that will diminish, not increase, our suffering. Without it we would remain tied to the wheel of samsara and gain nothing from this precious human form.

There has to be a strong motivation before we follow a spiritual path because our inborn inclination is to follow the dictates of selfishness instead. Therefore, as the desire to practise dharma leads to beneficial results, we should not worry in the beginning that this feeling is an attachment to be avoided. We should continue our practices with as pure a motivation as possible and in this way reap great benefits for all beings.

Thank you so much.

Part Two
A Meditation Course

6 The Three Principal Aspects of the Path to Enlightenment

Purification Visualization

We shall start off this morning with a short meditation in order to purify our minds and perhaps allow us to gain a better hold on the following teachings.

You should sit in your accustomed posture of meditation. If it is more comfortable to sit on a chair then this is perfectly all right. What is important is to gain control over the mind. This is facilitated if your back is as straight as possible and your shoulders level. Your eyes should be slightly open to allow some light in, but not too open in case distractions arise. As long as you do not become sleepy you may close them completely if you wish.

We begin by visualizing an infinite number of beings seated all around us looking forward. They will share with us whatever merit and benefit is to be gained from this purification meditation.

All are in the form of human beings and we should try to see the vast space around us completely filled with this assemblage.

Now let us visualize in the mind's eye, at the distance of about an armspan in front of us and level with our head, a large golden throne embellished with many jewels. When this image is clear, continue by visualizing a pure white lotus in full bloom resting upon this throne. This flower is immaculately bright and appears with no flaws or discolouration whatsoever. Inside the lotus are discs of first the sun and then the moon. These are placed one on top of the other like two round cushions. Upon this specially prepared seat sits Shakyamuni Buddha. Golden in complexion, he is in the form of a monk wearing saffron-coloured robes. His right hand is extended downwards touching the disc upon which he is seated and his left hand rests in his lap holding a begging bowl. Neither the form of Shakyamuni nor any other element of the visualization has even an atom of ordinary solid matter in it. Rather, everything we see is composed solely of brilliant, vibrant rays of pure light.

Think how Shakyamuni Buddha is a fully enlightened being completely purified of obscurations, every dualistic conception and all distorted views. His knowledge is perfected and he possesses a completely omniscient mind. He has the full power and the skilful means to lead each and every living being out of suffering by teaching pure paths to liberation and enlightenment. In his infinite compassion he desires to guide everyone, ourselves included, to the immediate cessation of all misery.

As he is able and willing to show us a way out of our problems, we should do our part by turning our mind to this source of wisdom, power and compassion. Therefore, holding the visualization as clearly as possible, each of us should make the following requests: "I am going to seek refuge in Buddha—the omniscient mind of Shakyamuni, in the dharma—his infinite knowledge and teachings, and in the sangha—those training their minds in accordance with his teachings. I am going to take refuge in and completely rely upon these three jewels until I myself reach enlightenment. Therefore, please grant help to me and to all living beings. Allow us to receive correct realizations of all the points of the graded path, from guru devotion up to the final achievement of full awakening."

Now visualize three syllables appearing on the form of Shakyamuni Buddha. These may be in Tibetan, English or in any other language. On his forehead appears a white *om,* on his throat a red *ah* and at his heart a blue *hum.* These syllables are also formed of light rays and are, respectively, the essence of the unsurpassable knowledge of a buddha's holy body, speech and mind. As white, red and blue light rays shine forth from these syllables they enter and purify us of all the negativities of body, speech and mind. When the white light from the *om* is received at our own forehead we should think that all the delusions, obscurations and negativities of the body are purified instantly and no longer exist anywhere. They have been completely obliterated. Similarly, the red and blue lights reaching our throat and heart cleanse us of all impurities of speech and mind so that we are entirely free of all negative karma. As this purification proceeds, we should experience the emptiness of all harmful and confused states of mind, feeling that these mental obscurations have been destroyed completely.

As the purifying lights stream out of the visualized buddha, we should recite the following prayer and then the mantra as many times as possible:

> Guru, founder,
> Fully realized destroyer of all defilements,
> One gone to thusness, foe destroyer,
> Perfectly completed buddha,
> Magnificent conqueror,
> Sage of the Sakyas —
> To you I prostrate and go for refuge,
> To you I make offerings.
> Please bestow your blessings on me.
> *Ta ya tha om muni muni mahamuniye svaha*

When we have finished this purification visualization, we should think that we have received the infinite knowledge of Shakyamuni Buddha's holy body, speech and mind. Try to feel this infinite bliss both physically and mentally and concentrate on it. Now that we have been purified, our entire body and mind should sing with a fully blissful nature. With such preparation we are now ready for the actual explanation of Buddha's dharma.

The Superiority of Spiritual Practice

At this time we are all engaged in a rather special activity that may be new to most of us. It is something we have not usually done in our daily lives. We are trying to find a practical method for solving our problems and allowing us to escape from suffering, but here we are looking at a method that is very different from any of the so-called solutions we have come up with in the past. At best, these other methods have granted us a short respite from misery; at worst they have led to an even greater dissatisfaction and frustration. However, here we are meeting a teaching in which it may be possible to place our full confidence, for by following it numberless beings in the past have achieved enlightenment. The same is true of the present time and will remain true in the future. This is the dharma method taught by the fully enlightened buddhas.

Dharma is something that cannot betray us. It is the antidote to the deceptive and misery-producing phenomena existing in samsara. These can and do betray us repeatedly. How does this happen? Without realizing their impermanence or the way in which they really exist, we trust them unquestioningly. Fooled by their superficial appearance, we place our faith in a completely distorted conception of these samsaric objects. Thus we react to our environment inappropriately and then feel betrayed when things do not turn out according to our expectations. This has been the pattern of our behaviour from beginningless lifetimes up to now. It has done nothing but lead us from one state of suffering existence into another.

It is obvious, when we consider how deeply engrained are our habits, that the dharma method cannot effectively lead us out of this circle of suffering if it is only practised occasionally. There will be no lasting benefit if we follow these teachings for a year or two or only when we journey to the East. It is something that should and can be done at all times, no matter where we are. We are living in an era when there is great danger not only from natural but also from man-made disasters. There is even less certainty than usual how much longer we can expect to retain this precious human body. Therefore it is important that we transform everything we do into the practice of dharma. We should not be content to fill our notebooks or our minds with merely an intellectualized account of the teachings. Rather, we must try to put everything we learn into practice immediately. In this way even the present activity of listening to a lecture can become an essential dharma activity, yielding especially beneficial results. It is not necessary for something to be physically or mentally difficult in order to be a valuable spiritual practice.

The profits gained in worldly pursuits do not begin to measure up to the benefits derived from dharma practice. We may find a particular occupation requiring advanced skills to be both financially rewarding and challenging, but these gains pale into insignificance when placed alongside those of spiritual training. Even if we were to acquire a universe of precious gems, we would still be unable to purchase enlightenment, personal liberation, the elimination of our delusions, an insight into the nature of reality, the enlightened motive of bodhicitta, a mind renouncing the sufferings of samsara or any of the many other attainments that derive from the practice of buddha dharma.

It ought not be surprising that material wealth and the like provide no real solution to our samsaric problems. Why is this so? If we collected in one place the vast amount of wealth we have already possessed during the infinite expanse of our past lives, the whole universe would be too small a vessel to contain it. Although these unimagineable riches have repeatedly been ours, they have been unable to buy us release from our sufferings. Our mind is still bewildered and confused enough to create problems for ourselves and others.

Through the practice of dharma, on the other hand, we can gain enlightenment and all the other beneficial attainments leading up to this supreme achievement. We can gain the satisfaction of a clear-sighted understanding of all inner and outer phenomena. Moreover, the sheer pleasure of dharma can never be exhausted nor can it change into an experience of pain. It is unceasing and provides us with continual happiness. Thus samsaric and dharmic pleasures are exact opposites. There was no beginning to our attempt at finding pleasure in samsaric activities, yet every instance of happiness gained from these came to an end sooner or later. If we look at our life closely, we shall find many examples testifying to the truth of this. The practice of dharma and the attainment of personal liberation and enlightenment, however, do have a discernible beginning in time, but the happiness they generate is without end.

Our main problem has been that we have lacked the discrimination and wisdom to understand what our experiences teach us about the nature of samsaric existence. Although worldly pleasures lead in the end only to disappointment and dissatisfaction, we remain ignorant of this fundamental truth and continue to chase after illusions of happiness. In this way the alluring aspect of samsara betrays us or, more accurately, we allow ourselves to be betrayed.

The essential dharma practice is to become aware of the consequences of our actions and thereby learn from our experiences. If we do this conscientiously, nothing can ever completely betray us and our mind can abide peacefully even in the midst of confusion. This is the way to reap great benefits not only for this life but for all future lives as well.

The main method to employ for transforming every activity into a dharma action is checking our motivation. This is a practical way of ensuring that everything we do will prove beneficial to ourselves and all others. If our motivation is established beforehand, whatever we do can definitely yield positive results. This is completely in accord with the actual workings of reality. Not only the evolution of samsaric sufferings, but that of enlightenment as well, is a creation of the mind. It is viewed by and arises only from the mind. Thus if we can maintain the proper motivation, the correct attitude of mind, we can be certain that whatever we do will lead to our attainment of enlightenment, the highest peace.

The Preciousness of our Human Form

The great Tibetan guru Je Tsong-khapa, who is the embodiment of the infinite wisdom of all enlightened beings, has said:

> The perfect human form, more precious than jewels,
> Is only to be gained at this present time.
> It is most difficult to find yet easily decays,
> Passing like a lightning flash in the sky.
> Thinking that such is the nature of life,
> It is necessary to take its essence
> Throughout the day and the night.
> I, the yogi, have practised like this.
> You who desire liberation please
> Train yourself in the very same way.

We have already indicated why our present form is far more precious than jewels or other wealth. It is only when we have a body favourably endowed with proper intelligence and sufficient leisure that we can achieve the fully enlightened state of a buddha, liberate ourselves from samsara and gain the many other advantages that with even all the wealth in the world we cannot hope to purchase.

Such a form is precious not only because it is so valuable but also because it is so rare to attain. Je Tsong-khapa has emphasized this point by stating that we can count on gaining it only once, "at this present time." This underscores the extreme difficulty of creating all the proper karmic causes resulting in a fully-endowed human birth. We must have amassed a great deal of meritorious karma to be born a human, and this is a difficult accomplishment. It is hard enough to act virtuously in our present state, but virtually impossible to do so in one of the lower, more unfortunate realms of existence where beings are totally preoccupied with pain. In the higher realms as well there is little time for virtue because the beings there are completely distracted by pleasure.

It is important to realize in addition that not every human has this precious form. There are many different circumstances that must be met before it can be considered fully purposeful. Externally, the teachings of dharma must be flourishing in a land we have access to and there must be well-qualified gurus there to guide us. Internally, we must have enough interest, desire and devotion to search out these teachings and put them into practice. In addition, we must be free of severe mental and physical handicaps that would make intensive dharma study and practice impossible. It requires a great deal of virtuous merit for all these many conditions to come about, and there is no certainty of gathering the necessary virtuous karma for such a form in the future. Therefore, Je Tsong-khapa advises us to consider this our final opportunity to make good use of this rare and precious endowment.

The opportunity presented by our attainment of a properly endowed human form can easily be lost, passing as quickly as "a lightning flash in the sky." The possibility that we may die at any moment is a very real one, yet we do not usually give it much thought. If we check inside ourselves we shall probably discover an intuitive belief that we shall live for a very long time. Even though the conditions leading to our death may come about before the day is through, we still hold onto the mistaken hope that we shall live nearly forever.

Such a wrong-minded view is one of the greatest hindrances to successful dharma practice because it leads to laziness and procrastination. Assuming that we shall remain alive a long time, we make excuses to ourselves for putting off serious study, meditation and practice. "I am tired now and in a bad mood, so I'll wait until tomorrow to follow the dharma . . . or maybe next week or next year." Such thoughts render useless whatever understanding we may have gained.

Perhaps we have heard all the proper teachings and are thoroughly familiar with the instructions for a particular meditation. If we continually put off actually taking the time to do this meditation, there will be no way for us to benefit from our information. The days will pass quickly, but there will be no change in our behaviour nor shall we gain any new realizations. We shall remain caught up in our familiar negative attitudes while making no progress whatsoever in the dharma. Then, before we realize it, this life will be over. We shall have lost this rare opportunity to gain release from cyclic existence and shall therefore die with great regret and self-reproach. Perhaps we shall live for a hundred years or more, but if we have not made any progress in the dharma, our death will still seem to come upon us like a lightning flash.

When we have meditated deeply on how valuable, rare and fragile our human form is, the thought should arise in our mind that worldly, samsaric activities have as little essence as a husk of grain. The more we meditate on these matters by looking into our own life and those of our acquaintances, the more we shall realize that lasting pleasure can only come from dharma practice. We can achieve our highest goals only if we make a sincere effort to tame our mind.

This brings us back to the question of motivation. By gaining control over our mind, and thus over our speech and body as well, we can avoid negative actions leading to a lower rebirth with much suffering. But, as we have discovered, even a rebirth in a more fortunate state of existence is not the solution to our problems. Certain rebirth realms may contain less of the obvious suffering of suffering than others, but the suffering of extensiveness pervades the entire samsaric universe. Therefore, if we want to overcome all pain, we must work towards our liberation from cyclic existence altogether.

Yet even this motivation is not the highest one. Numberless beings having the same longing for pleasure and dread of pain as ourselves are trapped in samsara. How can we think of gaining personal liberation when they are so deluded and helpless, lacking a teacher to guide them along effective paths to the cessation of their misery? Our motivation for practising dharma, therefore, should be nothing less than the enlightened motive of bodhicitta. We must work for our full enlightenment, an attainment that will enable us to help all beings out of their misery in the most effective way possible. Thus even such an activity as listening to this lecture can be transformed into an effective dharma practice if it is done with a pure bodhicitta motivation. The mere generation of this state of mind will have an inestimable effect on our eventual achievement of a fully awakened state.

The Fully Renounced Mind

If all the main points of the dharma were reduced to their essentials, they could be grouped into three categories commonly called the three principal aspects of the path to enlightenment. These are the fully renounced mind, the enlightened motive of bodhicitta and the correct view of emptiness (shunyata). Blended together they are like the fuel propelling our rocket to the moon of enlightenment. Thus it will be beneficial to organize the remainder of these lectures in terms of them. In this way it may be easier and quicker for us to subdue the negativities that have been plaguing us since beginningless time. Je Tsong-khapa has written a famous work on these three principal aspects, and I shall follow a commentary on it written by Kyabje Phabongkha Rinpoche, a great Tibetan ascetic lama recognized as having achieved oneness with the tantric meditational deity Heruka Chakrasamvara.

The gateway to all spiritual paths, whether leading to personal liberation or supreme enlightenment, is the fully renounced mind. Just as a passport, visa, vaccinations and sufficient money are necessary before we can undertake a long journey, so is this state of mind essential if we are to follow the dharma successfully. It often happens that even meditators in strict retreat find it difficult to make any progress in their practice. Despite the fact that they are in a conducive place and have received detailed instructions concerning their meditation, they are hampered by continual mental and physical hindrances. This is primarily because they have not developed a sufficiently powerful renounced mind. As soon as the strength of true renunciation increases, all such hindrances decrease automatically, and the meditations yield their fruit readily. The remedy, then, to our own difficulties in achieving significant realizations is also to develop such a mind.

Shakyamuni Buddha undertook his spiritual quest because he had developed a fully renounced mind. Thus he was able to cleanse himself of impurities, achieve omniscience and show countless beings, even today, paths to higher rebirth, liberation and enlightenment. Similarly, the satisfaction and pleasure experienced by the Tibetan yogi Milarepa while leading an ascetic existence, as well as his attainment of enlightenment in one lifetime, can be traced to his renunciation.

Contrary to the popularly-held belief that developing a renounced mind is a gloomy and pessimistic process, the meditators who work to achieve such an attitude experience great happiness even while in the midst of samsara. If we think that renunciation destroys all possibility of enjoyment in this life, we have not understood what this term means at all. When someone develops true renunciation he or she experiences far greater pleasure and enjoyment, both mental and physical, than someone who is surrounded by material luxury yet lacks such a realization.

Let us look into this matter more deeply. A person possessing such wealth may claim he is enjoying life to the fullest and that he therefore has no need of the dharma. He may say this even though his mind is subject to hatred, ignorance, pride, jealousy and so forth. If this is what he truly believes, how can we say he is suffering and claim that a yogi with a renounced mind is far happier? The reason is that a person caught up in finding pleasure and security in samsaric delights blinds himself, either consciously or unconsciously, to his negativities and the suffering he encounters. It is to protect his precarious state of mind that he refuses to admit the dissatisfaction he in fact does experience. Moreover he is unable to see that his delusions are in some way responsible for this. Therefore, his claim to be happy is superficial, for an honest evaluation reveals that he is not at peace at all. On the other hand, a meditator who has overcome such internal negativities by the strength of his renounced mind is thereby free of the misery caused by delusions and lives instead in true mental and physical comfort.

Physical problems arise from mental ones. Yet we do not usually consider such things as jealousy or desire to be forms of suffering. Only obvious afflictions such as bodily diseases are thought to be painful. However, it is precisely by this criterion of pain that all such mental negativities should be seen as suffering itself.

Consider the delusion of pride. Under its influence we are far from happy, but rather are quite ill at ease. We feel pumped up like an overinflated ballon. If we investigate, we shall see that this is quite an unpleasant sensation and that among its many consequences are physical nervousness and mental confusion. If we accept the fact that dis-ease is suffering, then surely we must include pride in this category.

It is very easy to see that anger too is a form of suffering. There is nothing comfortable about it. Anger generates a hardness in the heart, general restlessness and all the associated disadvantages of a cruel mind. Quite obviously it leads to nothing but pain.

The most difficult delusion to recognize as painful is greed. But this too is a disease. Let us suppose we are in a department store and see something we really like and desire to have. Our mind literally becomes stuck on this object and we cannot wait to own it. Whenever the memory of this object crosses our mind, we experience a peculiar tight sensation as if a sharp needle had been thrust into our heart. We may be in the habit of referring to this sensation as eager excitement, thinking it to be a form of pleasure, but a closer look should convince us that it is only another state of uneasiness.

In a similar fashion all the various mental afflictions and the actions they motivate are painful. The fact that someone might not recognize these negativities as a disease does not prove he or she is healthy. We can understand the truth of this by an example from medicine. It might happen that we go to the doctor for no special reason, but once there discover that something is drastically wrong with us. Our prior claim to good health is thus proven to be mistaken, and if we are wise we follow the doctor's treatment immediately. Thus if someone claims that his worldly existence is free of suffering and that dharma practice is only for crackpots and malcontents, perhaps it would be wise for him to investigate his defensive attitudes a bit more closely.

A fully renounced mind leads to enjoyment and happiness because the sources of confusion have been quieted. Developing such a mind does not mean becoming separated from the physical world and its enjoyments. If it did, then we could not possibly develop such a state until we had left our body, for it too is part of the physical universe. Nor does it mean that we should give up all our possessions. In a certain sense our mind is also a possession, and how can we ever hope to escape from it? Therefore renunciation is not an act of separation; it is not something we can accomplish by physical means. Rather, it is solely an action of the mind.

Then what exactly does such a mind renounce? We must develop renunciation of the *causes of suffering,* the mental afflictions themselves. Once we have given up these causes, problems cannot easily arise—either for oneself as an individual or for society as a whole and there is no way for pride, anger or greed to overwhelm us. We shall not run into trouble with either animate or inanimate objects because the source of all such difficulty has been removed.

It is important to repeat that renunciation does not imply that we should give up our enjoyments or possessions. There have been many highly realized beings who have been kings, wealthy merchants and the like. It is not our possessions but our ignorant, clinging attitude towards them that must be abandoned. Even if we are presently unable to work on these defiled attitudes, merely having an understanding of what renunciation means can be of great benefit in lessening our suffering. Of course, if we can actually develop such a renounced mind we shall achieve even greater results. We shall learn to deal with our possessions skilfully and thereby avoid all mental confusion. We shall develop the inner conviction of what renunciation means, seeing it as completely opposed to the mistaken belief that it leads to an unhappy, dreary life as an impoverished beggar.

The Renunciation of Suffering

Without having achieved the mind that fully renounces suffering, there is no way to escape from the ocean of samsara. We have been floundering in this ocean since beginningless time and shall continue to do so if we do not make the proper effort now to win our release. As the fully renounced mind is the foundation for the paths to liberation and enlightenment, it is taught before the enlightened motive or the correct view of emptiness

We cannot hope to develop renunciation if we do not first understand what samsara and suffering are. If we are unaware of the suffering nature of cyclic existence, we shall not be motivated to find a way out. Rather, we shall remain infatuated with temporary pleasures and shall consequently bind ourselves ever tighter to this wheel of suffering and dissatisfaction. We would thus be like the foolish prisoner who did not understand how miserable jail was in comparison to a life of freedom, and consequently took no advantage of opportunities to escape. Therefore, meditation on the nature of suffering is very important if we are to search for and follow a path to release from samsara.

Many people have very wrong conceptions about what samsara is. Some think it is a particular country, city, house, type of food or so forth. In connection with such mistaken views there is a story told in Tibet about the servant of a highly realized lama. He spent much of his time with this lama, serving him and managing his affairs. One day he decided to give up wearing the clothes of a layman and began dressing in robes instead.

Shortly thereafter he was sent on an errand to another great lama. His host thought that this servant must have acquired a great understanding of the dharma because he spent so much time with such an advanced spiritual master. So he asked him what progress he had made in his practices. "I have recently been released from samsara," the servant replied. The lama was overjoyed and asked how this came about. "Oh," the servant answered, "it was easy. I simply took off my pants!"

There are many similar misconceptions concerning samsara. Some people think once they are away from their normal surroundings and living in a cave or forest retreat that they have escaped from samsara. But this is not so, for even if we were to land on the moon we would still be in samsara. It is not a place we can escape from; it is a state of mind.

"Samsara" is a Sanskrit term meaning "circling" or "the round of existence." As long as we are caught uncontrollably in this circle of death and rebirth, we are still in samsara. At the moment, we are travelling through existence endowed with a precious human form. When this present life is over, our mind—or more accurately the continuity of our mental energy—will be blown without choice by the winds of our karma into another life. There it will inhabit yet another samsaric body. That life will also end and again our consciousness will have to move on involuntarily. This process will repeat itself forever unless we discover some way to escape.

What keeps us bound to the wheel of samsara? It is the karmic energy created by our actions together with the delusions motivating them. These two tie us to different samsaric bodies in the same way that ropes bind a prisoner to a post. The difference is that we ourselves knot this rope of karma and delusions; no one else imposes this suffering upon us.

As long as we continue to take rebirth in a samsaric body we shall continue to experience constant dissatisfaction and annoyance. Think of all the trouble we encounter merely because of our present form. We have to feed and clothe it and take great care so that it will stay healthy. We have to work in fields or factories to earn the money to support it, as well as build houses to keep it warm. After a hard day's work our mind feels depressed because our body is so tired. And yet no matter how much we try to protect ourselves, our body still manages to contract diseases and injure itself. Even though none of us wish to remain bound to such a source of discomfort, there appears to be no way for us to exist without it. This lack of freedom of choice is the very nature of samsara.

We cannot win our freedom by committing suicide. This unskilful action, born of despair, merely replaces one contaminated body with another. Rather, like the prisoner who cuts the ropes binding him, we must cut through our karma and delusions. Only in this way can we be free of having to take rebirth involuntarily. The motivation to sever these bonds comes from a deep understanding and beneficial dread of the sufferings found in all samsaric states of existence, not only those we have experienced in this life. Thus this meditation on renunciation must be expansive as well as deep.

There are many reasons why we should have as broad an outlook as possible. Every minute we perform hundreds of karmic actions and, depending upon their severity and frequency, they can throw us into many different types of existence. We need only take careful note of our mind when it is boiling with anger to gain a rough idea of the hellish karma we habitually create. If we were to die with our mind compressed and distorted by the root delusions, what kind of body would be a suitable vessel for such involuted conscious energy? Certainly not a fully endowed human form!

Furthermore, even with limited vision we can see that there are many forms of life besides the human, and there are many types of human life besides our own. There is no reason why the sufferings of an animal or a mentally deranged person could not come to us as well. Therefore, a fully renounced mind must encompass all states of existence, from the lowest imaginable to the highest. By doing proper examination meditation repeatedly, we shall not only develop complete renunciation but shall also experience the growth of great compassion for those unfortunate beings who are even now experiencing these terrible sufferings. Such compassion is very important, especially as we progress to higher stages of the path.

Shakyamuni Buddha taught that there are three states of existence lower than the human, and each is the karmic creation of the beings inhabiting them. These are the narak or hellish suffering realm, the preta or thirsting spirit realm, and the animal realm. Depending upon individual karma, the sufferings of these states can be experienced either in a particular physical location with a specific type of body or in the depths of the mind. In either case these sufferings are quite real to those who have collected the karma to experience them.

By developing deep insight into these unfortunate realms, we shall be motivated to renounce those non-virtuous actions responsible for such rebirths. It is far better to taste a few of those intense sufferings now in meditation, while there is still the chance to create counteracting good karma, than to remain unfearful of these realms until the day we find ourselves trapped there. Then it will be too late to do anything but wait out the agony of what might be an unbelievably long time.

If we think of these suffering realms in terms of the karma that lands us there, we can benefit greatly even in this life. For example, we may often become full of very proud thoughts and adopt an arrogant attitude towards our supposed inferiors. If, however, we understand that pride leads to a rebirth with horrible torment in one of the three lower realms of existence, and if we have experienced some of this pain in our meditation sessions, our mind will automatically let go of these harmful thoughts. The fear that makes the mind upset enough to stop creating further causes of misery is not a negativity. It is very beneficial. Something is negative only if it results in suffering. Therefore, as the fear of creating bad karma leads to a cessation of suffering, it is anything but negative.

The great Indian bodhisattva Shantideva has pointed out the benefits of meditating upon samsaric sufferings as follows:

> As a person remembers suffering he becomes upset
> And thereby loses his pride.
> And as he discovers his own samsaric suffering
> He will likewise discover that of other living beings.
> There is a chance, then, that compassion for them will
> arise.

Thus for ordinary beings like ourselves, who continually create negative karma and have a difficult time controlling our delusions, meditation on the sufferings of the lower realms is one of the best methods to develop a fully renounced mind.

The Six Realms of Samsara

The lowest rebirth realm is that of the narak or hell beings. We create the karma to experience its sufferings by harming or injuring others with cruel intentions. Fighting, killing and raping are some of the major non-virtuous actions resulting in a rebirth here. The narak realms may be either extremely cold or extremely hot, and rebirth in these hellish states is generally for an incredibly long time. According to one account, a rebirth in the least terrible of the hot naraks may last for nine billion human years!

Every moment in the life of narak beings is filled with pain. Some are compelled to battle with karmically created enemies. Each time they die they are revived, and the fight continues. The pain we would experience by having hundreds of spears thrust into our body does not begin to compare with the sufferings of these unfortunate beings.

As we go lower and lower into the narak realm, the suffering we experience grows and our lifespan increases twofold. At the lowest point in the hot naraks, the Avici Hell of uninterrupted pain, our suffering continues without a break and there is no way to tell our body from the fires that consume it.

Birth in a cold narak is like being trapped in a karmically created vision of ice and darkness. We are crushed within mountains of frozen rock. As storms arise and the temperature drops, our body begins to crack. Slowly it opens like a gigantic lotus and we turn blue and then red with the increasing cold. Karmically created insects and small animals come to feed at our open sores, but there is nothing we can do for we are frozen into immobility.

There are further descriptions that could be given, but we cannot go into them now. There are also similar narak sufferings experienced in the human realm. Accounts of all this can be found in several texts already translated into English. But when we read about or meditate upon these sufferings, we should not think that they are fantastic horror stories. Shakyamuni Buddha taught about these realms out of his knowledge and great compassion. He saw that beings actually do bring these torments on themselves and desired to show us ways of avoiding such horrible pain. If we dismiss these accounts as a weird fantasy and see no reason to change our behaviour, we shall be wasting this precious opportunity to escape from suffering altogether. We shall slip back into patterns of laziness and be forced to follow our mind wherever it is blown.

The next unfortunate realm is that of the pretas, the wandering spirits afflicted with great hunger and thirst. We can suffer their torments as the result of actions done under the strong delusions of greed, lustful desire and miserliness. A preta not only suffers from hunger and thirst but also from heat, cold, fatigue and fear. Above all, a preta's existence is filled with the torment of never being able to satisfy his or her overwhelming desires.

A preta may wander for many years without finding a drop of water. Should he discover some, it might disappear as he approaches. In the distance there seems to be a lake of clear blue water, yet when he hastens to it with great expectation he finds only mud and garbage. Should he be fortunate enough to find some water, there still are many obstacles preventing him from drinking it. His mouth is no larger than the eye of a needle and the scrawny neck leading to his cavernous stomach is tied in knots. The water often evaporates in his mouth or turns to acid upon reaching his stomach.

The lifespan of pretas is very long and must be measured in thousands of years. While their realm is located under the earth, many roam where humans and animals live. Certain people have the karma to be able to see pretas, but they are invisible to most of us. Yet we all have seen other human beings who are so caught up in miserliness and grasping that we cannot be sure to which plane of existence they actually belong.

Next is the animal realm. Birth here is largely the result of following brute instincts blindly and behaving with stubborn closed-mindedness. If we are born as an animal, we have virtually no opportunity to benefit ourselves. We spend nearly all our time unknowingly creating negative karma and stumbling into further suffering. If some kind human tries to teach us a mantra that is powerful enough to purify huge collections of negativities, we are too ignorant to do anything but beg food from him.

Most animals suffer greatly from hunger and thirst and from

the fear of being eaten by larger animals. Often when one captures something he devours it with great apprehension, continually looking around to avoid being killed himself by some other predator. Domestic animals may have the good fortune not to suffer from hunger like their brethren in the wild, but humans often mistreat them by forcing them to do difficult labour or tying them up as if they were in prison. In addition, there are many animals hunted and eaten by man, a far more ruthless and efficient enemy than other animals. We may have to use our imagination to empathize with the sufferings of narak beings and pretas, but the sufferings of the animal realm are there for all to see.

This concludes a very brief survey of the unfortunate realms. In addition, there are three other "fortunate" realms, so called because they afford varying amounts of samsaric pleasure. Thus one can also be born as a human, as an asura or titan, or as a deva, that is a god or goddess. Generally speaking, birth in these realms is the result of virtuous actions. However, since these are done under the influence of ignorance and with an impure motivation, we are still thrown uncontrollably into these samsaric realms by the forces of karma and delusion. The sufferings we experience here might be more subtle than those in the unfortunate realms, but they are still sufficient to fill us with dissatisfaction.

The devas occupy the highest level of samsara, possessing enjoyments of an almost dreamlike quality. These proud beings live in jewelled palaces where they indulge in every type of sensual pleasure. However, because they are so distracted by these delights, they make no effort to create any more good karma for themselves. All their time is spent using up the fruits of good karma collected in past lives. When they die, only negative karma is left and therefore most plunge directly into one of the unfortunate realms.

During the last week of a deva's life, said to last approximately 350 of our years, he or she experiences more mental anguish than a narak being ever does. He realizes he is going to die and can see the lower state into which he will be reborn. Other gods and goddesses, his previous companions, see his death signs and refuse to have anything more to do with him. Thus he is left alone, his lustre and once-beautiful flower garlands faded, awaiting his fall from glory.

The asura realm resembles that of the devas with whom they are always warring. Consumed by jealousy of the more lavish wealth of the superior devas, they are compulsively driven to plunder it. It is, however, nearly impossible for an asura to kill a deva, but he himself can be maimed or slaughtered quite easily by his foes. Thus jealousy prevents him from enjoying his own wealth and his attempts to acquire more are generally frustrated.

Finally we come to the human realm. We have already discussed the sufferings of birth, sickness, old age and death as well as those of being parted from what we like, meeting with what we dislike, frustration and dissatisfaction. Moreover, every misery experienced in the other five realms has its human counterpart. There are many more sufferings that can be mentioned, but we have time to consider only a few of the most pervasive.

One of our greatest torments is that we lack certainty about our possessions, attainments and our very status. We may spend a lot of time and effort acquiring something beautiful yet there is no certainty that its beauty will not fade or that we shall not lose it. In fact, about the only thing we can be sure of is that this object is impermanent and will eventually change and decay.

We should not betray ourselves by being attracted to such passing samsaric objects as our possessions, body or worldly pleasures. The problem does not lie in enjoying these objects while we have them, but in being attached to them. We should remember that we have possessed a universe of desirable objects in our past lives but none of them has helped us tame our mind or win release from suffering. We are still circling in samsara with no end in sight.

In all realms of cyclic existence we suffer from having to leave our body again and again. This is another aspect of uncertainty. To gain a rough idea of what this entails we should try to imagine as many members of our family tree as possible, that is our parents, their parents and so forth. What we can visualize is insignificant compared to the number of past lives each of us has led. In the same way that each of our forefathers was born, lived a short while and then died, so have we all taken birth again and again, giving up one body after another.

Even within the short space of a single lifetime we experience uncertainty as to our status. We may be president or king at one moment and an outcast or political prisoner the next. In Tibet, for instance, there were many rich people who probably thought they would always be wealthy. But within a short time nearly all of them lost their possessions if not their very lives.

Lastly, we should mention the suffering of loneliness. Although we exert great effort to surround ourselves with friends and companions, all the crises of life must be faced alone. We are born and die with no one to share our pain and worry. In all these ways, then, life in the six realms of samsara is fraught with misery. It is not pessimistic or fatalistic to think about suffering, but rather profoundly realistic. It is far better to face our troubles squarely and thereby find a way to break loose from them than to deny their existence and continue to suffer.

It is important to re-emphasize that none of the torments experienced in samsara are punishments applied from without. They were neither created by someone or something else, nor did they spring into existence by themselves. By our own thoughts, words and deeds we have arranged the causes and circumstances for our own suffering. As our karma changes so does each of the six realms. Neither the pleasures nor the pains of samsara have any definite, firmly established existence. Everything depends upon our changing mental attitudes. What *is* definite, however, is that non-virtuous actions result in suffering and virtuous ones in happiness. Therefore, we must try to avoid the former and practise the latter as much as possible.

We cannot hope to break out of the wheel of samsara until we realize that alluring pleasures are merely a disguised form of suffering. And we cannot gain this realization until we develop a dread of samsara in general and the unfortunate realms in particular. We must understand vividly that if our behaviour is motivated by delusions, we shall have to pay a heavy karmic debt in suffering, both now and in the future. The biggest obstacle preventing us from realizing this is our complusive attraction to samsaric pleasures. Attachment can be likened to oil. It is very hard to remove such a stain from a piece of paper. Moreover, dust and grime adhere to the oil, dirtying the paper even more. In a similar fashion, attachment pollutes our mind and attracts other delusions to it. The best way to free ourselves from this delusion is to remember samsaric suffering and thereby develop a mind that renounces its causes.

If we were to fear the defilements of hatred, attachment, ignorance and so forth as much as we dread a raging fire, we would be able to protect ourselves from harm. In nearly every building there is a fire extinguisher. What motivates someone to place it there? It is a vivid understanding of how destructive fire can be. Knowing that an extinguisher protects him from this danger, a householder can then proceed with the tasks of his daily life. In the same way, fear of suffering and renunciation of its causes allow us to make the best use of this precious human form.

Imagine two friends eating ice cream cones. One, whose mind is untrained, devours his with great attachment and desire. Nearly every swallow marks the creation of one type of negative karma or another. His mind, tossed back and forth between expectation, greed, frustration and disappointment, is so preoccupied that he often misses a great deal of the ice cream's pleasant taste. His friend, on the other hand, who has had some experience meditating on the suffering nature of samsaric pleasures, eats his cone slowly and peacefully. He does not let attachment arise to mar his enjoyment of it. Since his mind is unhindered by delusions, he can even transform this simple activity into a pure dharma practice. Thus he can derive temporal and ultimate happiness from something that brings his friend dissatisfaction and discomfort. As this example demonstrates, a fully renounced mind brings us enjoyment not only when we are released from samsara but while we are still within it.

How We Create Samsara

We have already stated that we are blown from one samsaric realm to another by the winds of our karma and delusions. And we have also shown what results to expect from creating karma while under the influence of different defilements. Perhaps it would now be useful to give a brief account of the actual mechanism that transports us from one life to the next.

This mechanism is the chain of interdependent origination, having twelve links: (1) ignorance, (2) karmic formations, (3) consciousness, (4) name and form, (5) the six sense faculties (6) contact, (7) feeling, (8) craving, (9) grasping, (10) becoming, (11) rebirth and (12) ageing and death. As Nagarjuna, the great propagator of Shakyamuni Buddha's wisdom-teachings, has said:

> Within the twelve links
> There are three delusions
> And two actions (karma).
> The remaining seven are the result.

The delusions are (1) ignorance, (8) craving and (9) grasping, and the actions are (2) karmic formations and (10) becoming. The remaining seven are the results experienced in a future rebirth.

A chain of interdependent origination describes the process of rebirth from one suffering state of existence into another and thus cannot be completed in one life, but requires either two or three. Taking as an example our present birth as a human, this process might be briefly explained as follows.

In a past life while under the all-pervading influence of (1) ignorance of the true nature of reality, we performed actions of body, speech and mind that impressed many (2) karmic formations or seeds of karmic instinct onto our (3) consciousness or mind. Some of these actions were sufficiently virtuous, however, to create the karma for rebirth as a human. Thus sometime during this first life we completed one delusion, one action and part of one result. We say "part" because the consciousness link has two divisions: causal and resultant. The former is our mind in a past life receiving impressions of karma, as in our example, while the latter is our mind thrown into its next rebirth.

When that first life approached its end, we experienced great insecurity and an intense fear of dying. By (8) craving and (9) grasping both for the body and possessions we were leaving behind as well as for a new body to replace the one we were vacating, we set into motion (10) becoming, the force leading to the coming into existence of another life. Thus at the time of death we completed two more delusions and one more action, thereby activating karmic seeds to be reborn a human being.

The remaining seven links occurred during this present life. Our (3) resulting consciousness was conceived in a human mother's womb where it joined with sperm and egg. From this embryonic combination of (4) name and form—"name" referring to the various potentialities of consciousness and "form" to the fertilized egg—there developed (5) the six sense faculties followed by (6) contact with sensory objects eventually eliciting (7) feelings of happiness, unhappiness or indifference in relation to those objects. Everything that has happened since the moment of conception forms part of (11) the rebirth link of this lifetime. From the second moment onwards we have begun to grow older, undergoing the various changes and sufferings described earlier. Thus part of (12) the ageing and death link is already completed and all that is left is for us to pass away.

This process can also take three separate lifetimes to complete with many years conceivably intervening between the first two. Consider the karma we may be creating at this very moment. It might be especially virtuous but done in (1) ignorance of the way things really are, for example with strong I-consciousness or ego-grasping. This ignorance may be planting (2) karmic formations in our (3) consciousness for us to be reborn as a glorious deva.

Now it might happen that at the time of our death the karma to be reborn a deva will not be as strong as the karma collected at some other time for rebirth as a dog. Thus the (8) craving, (9) grasping and (10) becoming links that come into play as we die will be of another chain of interdependent origination. The karma to be reborn as a deva, however, is not lost. It is still carried in our consciousness but will not be activated until some future death. In our very next life we shall experience the seven remaining links as a dog. Eventually, however, the deva karma will come to the fore and the three links at death and the seven of the following life will unfold as explained above.

This is an abbreviated account of the process of rebirth, but it is sufficient to give us a good idea of how many chains we have been forging and continue to forge through our ignorance. When we plant seeds in a field, what grows is far greater than what was sown. Similarly, the constant stream of tiny karmic seeds we plant in our mind will produce suffering results completely out of proportion to their cause. Every minute of every day for countless lifetimes we have been acting under the influence of the major and minor delusions. Thus we have accumulated enough karma to be reborn into each suffering realm many times over. We have forged the first three links of an infinite number of chains and unless we tame our mind, guard our behaviour and eliminate our ignorance, we shall be hauled by these chains into one suffering existence after another. Our mind is like the baggage car of a railway train. It goes from place to place and life to life collecting parcels of karma that must some day be delivered and paid for.

Samsara is a prison we have fashioned ourselves in which we are surrounded by a vast net of concentric fences keeping us trapped in our ignorance. We complete one chain of twelve links and climb over one of these fences only to find that we are still in the centre of many others. Thus samsara will not come to an end by itself. We cannot hope to exhaust it by passing through life creating more and more karma. We shall only win our release when we cut through the root and source of these links, our ignorance of the true nature of reality.

As we mentioned before, the development of a fully renounced mind depends on our recognition of the all-pervading suffering of extensiveness. This is the misery of having an uncontrolled, contaminated body that produces suffering naturally. We should not think that first we are born and only afterwards create and experience the discomforts of life. As the discussion of the twelve links demonstrates, the process of rebirth takes place *with* suffering. Our consciousness receives the imprints of karma and is thrown into its future rebirth in a state of profound dissatisfaction and uneasiness. We say that samsaric beings have a contaminated or deluded body precisely because consciousness enters it involuntarily, thrown by the forces of karma and delusion.

No sooner does our body come into existence than it begins to die. Some beings meet their death in the womb after a very short time. Yet even those of us who live much longer have a life span made up of a certain number of minutes and seconds. As each second passes by, we move that much closer to our death. We are like a sheep which is being taken from the field to the slaughterhouse. With every step it takes it comes nearer to its end.

If we learn to view all realms of samsaric existence as suffering, there will be no chance for attachment to arise for worldly pleasures. This is very important as it opens the way for us to develop the correct view of emptiness, cut through the root of samsara altogether and attain liberation. Even if we do not progress this far along the path, a fully renounced mind is very beneficial at the time of death. Because we have done much death meditation beforehand, we shall have a good idea of what to expect and will not fall prey to confusion and worry. Also, as we are unattached to existence in samsara, we shall be far less likely to crave and grasp for a new rebirth. Thus we can avoid being reborn not only in one of the three unfortunate realms but anywhere in samsara. If we have enough control over our mind and do not activate any attachment or aversion at all, we can be reborn in a pure land without being forced to take a contaminated body. There we can progress unhindered towards our goal of liberation and enlightenment.

What then is the sign that we have developed true renunciation? As Je Tsong-khapa has said:

> Whenever there is no interest or attachment
> for even a second to samsaric pleasures,
> And the thought seeking liberation
> Arises day and night—
> Whoever has developed such a mental state
> Has achieved the realization of the fully renounced mind.

The Advantages of an Enlightened Motive

Je Tsong-khapa has shown the connection between the preceding sections and what follows by stating:

> The fully renounced mind of samsara by itself
> Without the enlightened motive of bodhicitta
> Cannot become the cause
> Of the perfect happiness of full enlightenment.

As he says, if we are to achieve the supreme goal of buddhahood, our fully renounced mind must possess the thought of bodhicitta —the motivation to become enlightened for the benefit of all living beings. Some people mistakenly believe that they can practise true bodhicitta without renunciation. But this is not possible. They probably think this way because bodhicitta sounds like a pleasant practice that does not require us to give up anything, whereas renunciation seems much more austere and difficult. Unfortunately, this is not really so. The development of bodhicitta involves many progressive stages of meditation requiring great seriousness and dedication. It is not simply a matter of thinking kind thoughts.

The benefits of bodhicitta, however, are well worth any trouble involved in attaining it. It is the gateway to the Mahayana path and whoever develops it is worthy of being called the son or daughter of the victorious Buddha. If we possess the bodhicitta motivation we surpass in glory even the arhats, those magificent beings who have gained liberation from samsara but are not yet striving towards full enlightenment. These lower arhats possess incredible psychic powers and other wonderful attainments, but someone who has bodhicitta—that is, a bodhisattva—is far more worthy of offerings than they.

The greatest benefits of bodhicitta appear in terms of our actual dharma practice. Every spiritual action we perform becomes more powerful and effective when done with an enlightened motive. For example, it is said that giving a handful of food to a dog, if done with bodhicitta, brings us more benefit than giving a universe of jewels to every living being without such a motivation.

Thus it is not the material of our offerings, or the status of the recipient, or even the specific practice we follow that determines how far or fast we progress along our path. Rather, as with everything else, it is our state of mind that is of primary importance. As bodhicitta is the highest possible motivation, it empowers our actions to a far greater extent than our ordinary selfish impulses.

Even without an actual realization of bodhicitta, if we possess a similar selfless attitude, it will eventually lead to this higher motive and, in the process, be very beneficial for our practice. Therefore, whether we are helping people, reciting texts, burning incense or merely eating, talking or engaging in business—whatever we are doing becomes an essential dharma practice if we dedicate it towards our attainment of enlightenment for the sake of others.

The ripening of negative karma keeps us circling within the six realms of samsaric existence. Thus it is our most dangerous enemy, causing us continual suffering. Bodhicitta has the unsurpassable power to purify such negative karma, freeing us from having to experience the results of our deluded actions. As the great bodhisattva Shantideva has said:

> The negative karma of the five heinous crimes
> Leads us to aeons of suffering in the hell called Avici,
> Yet the realization of bodhicitta
> Can purify this karma in a very short time.

The external hindrances interrupting our practices are also overcome by the power of bodhicitta. To quote Shantideva once again:

> If we subdue our mind
> We shall subdue as well
> The tiger, snake and elephant
> And all such frightening beasts.

This is not an empty poetic sentiment but a statement of fact. There are many stories and eye-witness accounts of the ability of bodhicitta and similar altruistic motives to protect people from harm. Many great bodhisattvas of India and Tibet had to make journeys through jungles inhabited by the fiercest animals. Yet it often happened that these animals would become subdued when these bodhisattvas approached. It was as if even these creatures knew enough to pay respect to such spiritual masters. Even normally timid creatures, such as birds and deer, would approach to see what manner of beings they were. Similar occurrences have been the experience of present-day meditators as well.

Lastly we should mention that the development of bodhicitta allows us to enter the lightning vehicle of tantra, the quickest path to the attainment of enlightenment. We need to have developed a firm experience of renunciation and be familiar with the correct view of voidness before we can enter the tantric path. But most especially, we must have a very strong bodhicitta motivation. Unable to bear seeing other living beings experience their over-whelming suffering, we must long with all our heart to gain buddhahood as quickly as possible for their benefit. If we engage in tantric practices with such a motivation, we can achieve our goal in one short lifetime. Without it, expecting results from even the most profound tantric teachings is like waiting for the moon to fall out of the sky.

If we examine the advantages and benefits of bodhicitta and understand the goal it leads to, it will become clear that the enlightened motive is the field from which all living beings reap their happiness. When someone develops bodhicitta he or she be-comes a source of true joy for all. There is no limit to the benefits he bestows on others and no way to measure the extent of his influence. Thus it is extremely worthwhile to exert great effort in practising the meditations leading to such a powerful attainment.

Achieving Equilibrium

The motivation to gain full enlightenment and thereby be able to lead all beings out of their suffering arises once we have seen that it is our responsibility to help others as much as we can. We can gain such a realization only after we have developed compassion, the wish to see everyone freed from his or her suffering. This in turn depends upon the growth in us of pure love, the desire to see others happy. Such love will arise only if we remember the kindness of all motherly beings and therefore wish to repay it. And finally, we shall not be able to recognize everyone as our benefactor if we harbour partiality for some and aversion for others. Therefore, as it is very important to maintain an unbiased attitude towards all, we should first practise equanimity or equilibrium meditation.

There are three objects of this meditation: friends, enemies and strangers. How do such labels arise? Because we are so preoccupied with ourselves, with our "I," we become very attached to our body, possessions, comforts and the like. Anyone who interferes with these or threatens our happiness is immediately labelled "enemy." Likewise, if someone does something to increase our happiness, he or she quickly becomes a "friend." As for strangers, they are those who give us neither help nor harm, and we therefore tend to ignore them completely.

The foundation of equilibrium meditation is to see how senseless and disadvantageous it is to make such discriminations. The attitudes of hatred, attachment and closed-minded ignorance that arise in us when encountering others in terms of these fixed labels are highly detrimental to ourselves and others. The wish to destroy enemies and defend friends has been the cause of all the many conflicts in the world, from squabbles between two individuals to global war. All this negative karma and suffering would come to an end if everyone could see how baseless such partisanship really is.

First of all, we must realize that attachment is at the root of all judgements we make as to enemy, friend and stranger. We are attached either to threatened possessions, people who have helped us or our own ignorant view of who is important to our wellbeing. The disadvantages of this clinging attitude have been described in detail before. It is necessary here only to be reminded that the "I" experiencing such attachment is a completely distorted conception of an ignorant mind.

Secondly, nothing is certain in samsara, including these three classifications. There is no such thing as a definite enemy, someone who has always harmed us and will always continue to do so. Thinking about our infinite number of past lives and about the ever-changing pattern of relationships in samsara should convince us that our present enemy was once our dearest friend, and vice versa. It is not even necessary to rely on an argument based on past lives to realize how often the status of friend, enemy and stranger changes. Where is our best friend from childhood now and what had we previously felt towards the relative we now find so annoying? It is very beneficial to do intensive examination meditation on this point, concentrating on specific individuals we classify in these three ways and trying to visualize them with altered status. As we become increasingly familiar with such meditation we should try to expand its scope, including in it more and more beings and thinking in terms of longer ranges of time. In this way we shall overcome many of the restrictions of our previously near-sighted views.

Repeated practise of equilibrium meditation will make us wary of accepting as valid our prejudiced opinions of others merely because these are our accustomed thoughts. As a result we shall be in a far better position to intercept our negative thoughts, words and actions towards others before they cause great harm. The more we practise such meditation the less likely we shall be to fight, act possessively or behave inconsiderately towards others. For instance, if we find ourselves becoming angry with someone, we can dissolve our hatred immediately by remembering this meditation. In this way we can convincingly prove to ourselves that there is nothing valid or ultimate about our biased attitudes. They are merely the product of closed-minded ignorance and with spiritual practise can be dispelled, bringing peace.

Remembering the Kindness of our Many Mothers

An experience of inner peace, which is a significant achievement in itself, is not the main purpose or benefit of equilibrium meditation. By learning to look at all living beings without bias, we are in a position to appreciate the kindness we have received from each of them. With such a realization we can overcome all selfishness, even that involved in working for our personal liberation from samsara.

Whenever we see or think about our mother—or about someone who has taken exceptional care of us—there is an automatic recognition of who she is and a certain strong feeling arises within us. When we have practised equilibrium meditation and gained some appreciation of the continuity of lives, we learn to respond to all beings in the same way. Each of them has been a mother to us in the past and, as such, has shown us immeasurable kindness.

Thinking first about the mother of our present life is the best way to progress in our development of bodhicitta. Her kindness to us started while we were still in her womb. With great selflessness she underwent many privations and subjected herself to strict discipline in order to protect us from harm and discomfort. She was very careful about what she ate or drank, how she walked and what kind of clothing she wore.

Even though our birth caused her great discomfort and pain, this did not reduce the affectionate care she displayed towards us. When we were infants she looked after us twenty-four hours a day and did everything in her power to keep us from harm. We were not an easy burden for her, always crying and soiling our clothes, but she comforted and cleaned us time and time again. Even when she was eating, her thoughts were concerned with our welfare. If she found a particularly delicious piece of food on her plate she would often give it to us. Even nowadays, we do not take care of ourselves with a fraction of the devotion that she displayed.

As she watched us grow older, her thoughts turned towards our future. It was her fondest wish that we be happy and lead a successful life. She worried a great deal about our education, often teaching us the rudiments of reading and writing herself. In fact, our ability to do many things as effortlessly as we do now owes a lot to her attention and interest. In typically near-sighted fashion we think that our powers and abilities are solely our own accomplishment. "Everything I have I worked for myself," we think. Yet had our mother neglected us for even one day while we were young, we would not even be alive much less functioning competently. Even now, when we run into problems, there is usually one person we can count on to help us to the extent of her abilities.

In addition, our mother is often our greatest admirer. If we do something good she is filled with delight and often exaggerates our accomplishments. She wants us to have a good reputation and is sometimes willing to lie about us to others in order to gain it. In short, there are many things that our mother has done for us throughout our life and the vast majority were done in complete selflessness. From whom else could we possibly expect such devotion?

If we expand our perspective to include our past lives, we shall see that this is not the first time she has been our mother. Many times in various realms of existence she has cared for us with at least equal intensity. For instance, there have doubtless been times when she was a mother hen and we her baby chick. As such, she spent a lot of time keeping her nest warm and digging up food for us. Even though a hen is normally a very cowardly creature, if she felt we were in any way endangered, she was prepared to sacrifice her own life for our sake. Our meditation on the kindness of motherly love can be expanded by thinking of many such examples from the animal realm. Then we should expand this further by remembering that at one time or another during our countless past lives *every* being has been our mother, caring for us at least as much as our present parent.

Our fellow creatures have been kind to us not only when they were our mothers, but at other times as well. We can review the events of an entire day, counting up each experience of pleasure and none will be found that did not depend to some extent on others. Each plate of food we have eaten involved the labour of many farmers, transporters, packagers and store-keepers. Nor should we neglect to consider all the tiny creatures who lost their lives during the planting and harvesting of this food. If we take the time to think this matter through carefully, we shall see that our lives and those of every being on this planet are intricately inter-woven.

Our ability to practise the dharma and gain insight into the nature of reality is also due to the kindness of other beings.

Everything depends on others, from our attainment of a precious human form and the leisure to use it wisely, to our development of a fully renounced mind, bodhicitta and the correct view of voidness. Why is this so? Each one of these attainments is the product of both the good karma we ourselves have created and that of the many enlightened beings who have taught the spiritual paths of the dharma. Both sets of karma were created in dependence upon other beings. For example, a buddha's achievement of enlightenment stems largely from his or her development of bodhicitta. This in turn is dependent upon compassion, love and so on felt towards others, all growing out of equilibrium meditation. Thus at every stage of his development, the would-be buddha depends upon other living beings. They provide him with all his opportunities to practise generosity, patience and so forth, and thus are directly responsible for all his subsequent achievements.

When we remember the kindness of the enlightened beings in showing us true paths to the cessation of suffering and see how their ability to do so depended in turn upon the kindness of each and every living creature, we shall lose whatever reason we had for becoming angry with anyone. How can we possibly hate even our most harmful enemy if he has played such an important role in bringing us both samsaric and ultimate happiness? Every pleasure experienced in the past, present and future is traceable to him. Thus, even while he is behaving badly towards us we should feel great compassion for him. This one-time mother of ours is suffering enough from delusions without us having to confuse matters even more by generating hatred towards him. Compassion is a transcendent Mahayana virtue only when it encompasses *every* being equally. We cannot hope to achieve bodhicitta if we wish to free only some people from their suffering.

If we develop enough perseverance and insight to regard even our worst enemy as a precious treasure mine to be cherished and protected, a great deal of confusion will be banished from our mind. Hatred and anger, which can destroy aeons of good karma in a single moment, can scarcely arise in a mind that dwells on the kindness of all motherly beings. But the only way to test the truth of these teachings is to practise them ourselves. It may take a long time to reach the stage where we can view every sentient being as our kind mother, but even before such an achievement we should experience deep inner satisfaction and peace of mind. If this happens we shall know that we are on a correct spiritual path.

Benefiting Others

Once we have brought to mind the many kindnesses we have received from others, we should consider what would be the best way to repay them. Giving them food and clothing is indeed helpful and if it is within our power we should certainly practise such charity. We should not neglect to do anything that might be beneficial to others. However, it is very important to realize that no material gift has the power to cut through the root of all suffering. The most it can do is offer temporary relief. If we really want to repay the infinite kindness of others, we must do so in an inner spiritual way. Only such a method can bestow the fruits of true, lasting peace and happiness on others.

However, we shall be unable to offer help to others if we have not cleansed our mind of its most disabling afflictions. The greatest obstacle towards working for the benefit of others is our deep-rooted self-cherishing attitude. Thus if we are sincere in wishing to repay others' kindness, we must try to uproot this self-centred attitude completely.

There is no reason why we should constantly place our own welfare above that of others or feel that we are of primary importance. As it says in the profound tantric text, the *Guru Puja:*

Please bless me and each sentient being to think continually
That all others should have happiness and its cause,
For there is not the slightest difference between myself
And all other beings who never find satisfaction
Nor desire even the smallest suffering.

Despite the fact that no one wants pain and everyone wants happiness, we have been behaving as if we were the only ones in the world who mattered. Since beginningless time we have been looking out for only ourselves, but what has this brought us?

Certainly none of the higher spiritual achievements. It has only led us to commit aggressive and defensive nonvirtuous actions, and we are still not through experiencing their harmful karmic results. Thus it would be wise to take advantage of the precious opportunity of this rebirth and the teachings we have received by beginning to cherish others instead.

The *Guru Puja* stresses the importance of exchanging our self-cherishing attitude for one of cherishing others by saying:

> Please bless me to be able to change myself into others
> And to equalize myself with them
> By thinking about the benefits and shortcomings
> Of the following actions:
> A buddha works only for others
> While the small-minded child works only for himself.
>
> To cherish oneself brings only downfall,
> And to hold dear our mothers
> Is the basis of all that is good.
> Therefore by the practice of exchanging self for others,
> Please bless me to be able to do all of this.

The consequence of exchanging self for others is that we grow much more aware of the predicament of all living beings. We remember what they have done for us in the past and are therefore determined to relieve them of as much suffering as we can. As the feelings of love and compassion for others grow even stronger, nothing makes us happier than sympathetic joy in another's pleasure and nothing sadder than someone else's misery. When we have an experience of pleasure we automatically think of sharing it with those less fortunate. Likewise, when we see others in pain we wish we could bear this burden for them. If we can actually share our happiness or take on others' pain, this is excellent. However, even if we cannot, the wish to do so plants many seeds that will someday ripen in our ability to bring others infinite happiness and joy. As Shantideva points out:

> A kindly person who thinks to cure
> The headaches of all beings acquires

By this good intention infinite merit.
How much more is acquired by someone
Wishing to alleviate the countless aches of all beings,
Wanting them to create infinite virtue!

When we compare ourselves with others, the main difference we now note is that we have had the good fortune to hear teachings concerning the taming of the mind. After a little meditational practice we experience freedom from many negativities that had previously plagued us. Other beings have not been so fortunate. They still wallow in their delusions and have no guide to lead them out of their continual misery. Although they all wish to be happy, their every action brings them only more pain. As this perception grows in clarity and vividness, we develop the pure wish to be able to lead all these suffering beings onto true paths to freedom. We regret any pain we have caused them in the past and become interested only in ways to make them happy.

We become like the dutiful child who takes on the responsiblility of helping his mother through difficult times. We cannot bear the thought that others must face their incredible suffering. We feel something must be done and we are the only one to do it. Yet when we look inwards we realize that we barely have the ability to help ourselves, much less all others. We therefore search to find someone who is able to do all this, thinking to emulate that person. Then we come to see that only fully enlightened beings— those who have followed the spiritual path to completion and have attained the exalted state of complete awakening, buddhahood— have the power to lead each and every being out of suffering. When all these realizations come together and we are determined to win for ourselves full enlightenment for the sake of benefiting all motherly beings, we have developed true bodhicitta, the enlightened motive.

This concludes the discussion of the development of bodhicitta, the second of the three principal aspects of the path to enlightenment. Whether or not we have created any merit during this lecture is solely an individual matter, depending on the attitude of each person here. If there has been any merit generated, we should dedicate it immediately for our own and everyone else's attainment of enlightenment. In this way any good karma we have created will not be destroyed or perverted by negativities.

Think that our virtues of the past, present and future and our present bodies, possessions and wealth are all offered to the enlightened beings, bringing them infinite bliss. Then these accumulations should be dedicated to every living being until there is nothing left for us to cling to as our own. Think of every offering as a source of realization whereby all creatures can progress through the entire spiritual training of dharma and achieve the most supreme goals. Then think that every being has become fully enlightened, purified of even the most subtle delusion. Finally, pray that by whatever merits we have created today we shall all quickly achieve insights into the three principal aspects of the path to enlightenment. Thank you very much.

Perceiving the Nature of Reality

Each and every meditational dharma practice has been taught for only one reason: to lead beings to the correct view of reality—that all things are empty of independent self-existence. If we develop a faultless understanding of the true way in which all things exist, we can gain personal liberation from the samsaric wheel of suffering. Ignorance is the root link in the chain of misery dragging us involuntarily to repeated birth, death and rebirth in samsara. With wisdom we cut through this ignorance and thereby free ourselves from the chains of our karma completely. Moreover, if we attain such wisdom while in possession of the enlightened motive of bodhicitta, we shall achieve not merely personal liberation but the omniscience of full awakening. Then we shall be fully able to lead all motherly beings to their desired cessation of suffering as well.

In order to understand emptiness (shunyata), we must become acquainted with unmistaken teachings on this subject. Such were taught by Shakyamuni Buddha and have been passed down to the present day by an illustrious unbroken lineage of meditators and pandits including such outstanding figures as Nagarjuna, Chandrakirti and Je Tsong-khapa. If we follow divergent teachings that do not explain the ultimate nature of things, we shall never be able to perceive the true nature of reality no matter how much we may meditate. Thus it is very important to search out correct explanations and then study, think about and meditate upon them well. What follows outlines the teachings of these great Indian and Tibetan gurus.

Je Tsong-khapa has said:

> One who can see the cause and result
> Of all existence within samsara and liberation
> As unbetraying, and whose false view is dissolved,
> Has entered the path that pleases the buddhas.

The wisdom of emptiness should be a direct remedy for our ignorance of the true nature of reality. If this wisdom is not completely opposite to the ordinary way we view things, then it is not true wisdom at all. Because our ignorance conceives of objects in a distorted manner, our wisdom must be directly opposed to it in order to be effective. Thus, first we must gain insight into how our perception normally functions so we shall know what we must combat.

Our mind has been so accustomed to viewing things in a distorted manner that it is difficult to gain a clear picture of reality. Because our wisdom is so limited, it is hard enough to recognize our mistaken beliefs, much less the actual state of things. For instance, if we ask ourselves, "What exactly is this 'I' that I am always talking about?" we shall have great difficulty in formulating an answer. This is so despite the fact that we think in terms of "I" at all times, even in our dreams. Our delusions are so thick that we cannot even explain what we are accustomed to seeing.

From beginningless samsaric lifetimes up until now we have been thinking of our "I" as if it were something inherently unique, born by itself and existing completely independently. It does not appear to rely on our body, mind or anything else. Rather, it seems to be completely self-sufficient. We did not have to learn this erroneous belief; we are born, die and born again with it instinctively. In fact, the very reason we take birth in a contaminated body is that our mind is preoccupied with the supposed self-existence of this "I," and we therefore crave and grasp for security on its behalf.

This way of looking at ourselves is completely mistaken. For example, when we are frightened or angry, the strong feeling, "*I* don't like this at all!" arises within us and everything else becomes unimportant. The only thing we can think about is how to defend this apparently self-existent "I" lodged in our heart. But, in fact, such a supposedly independent "I" has no real existence whatsoever. It is the product of a completely ignorant conception.

There is a conventional "I" that we *do* have, but the fact that it exists in one way while we believe it to exist in a completely contrary manner is the principal source of all our suffering. We are constantly running into problems of our own making because our expectations are based on a false idea of who we are. Our judgements are mistaken and we are unable to deal skilfully or effectively with the situations we encounter. No wonder we are always disappointed by the way things turn out and experience great discomfort and dissatisfaction as a result.

Why is it wrong to feel that the "I" is some sort of independent entity existing by itself? If we approach this question carefully, the answer will eventually become clear. It is impossible to think of the "I" without also thinking in some way of either the mind or the body. Thus, if the "I" were truly independent and self-sufficient, it would either have to be exactly the same as the body and mind, existing in perfect oneness with them, or else be something totally separate and distinct from either. If we meditate on this well, we shall see that these are the only two possibilities.

However, it is obvious that the "I" cannot exist separately from the body and mind because there is no "I" we can point to without also pointing to some aspect of our mental or physical make-up. For example, when the body is sleeping we say, "*I* am asleep." When it is engaged in consuming food we say, "*I* am eating." When it is resting in a chair we say, "*I* am sitting." If the "I" actually did exist in the way we instinctively conceive it to—as something independent of our body or mind—then it would be meaningless to refer to our activities in such ways. If the "I" were something that existed separately from the body, why should we think "I am sitting" when our body is in a chair?

The same holds true with respect to the mind. In a very short space of time our mind engages in many different, and often contrary, activities. Yet whether the mind is thinking, sleeping, meditating, becoming angry or merely dreaming, we say "*I* am thinking," "*I* am meditating," "*I* am angry," and so forth. If there were an "I" that existed in some way separately from these various states of mind, it would be senseless to refer to all these mental activities in terms of an "I" felt to be unique and independent.

The only remaining alternative concerning a supposedly independent "I" is equally mistaken. This is to think that it is the same as the body, mind or one of their aspects. Such a view cannot stand up to analysis either. Despite the fact that the label "I" refers in some way to the body and mind, there is no one part of our physical or mental make-up that we can point to and say, "This is 'I'." Neither our hand, nor our heart, nor any other part of our body is our "I." Nor can we say that what we are thinking or feeling at this or that moment is our "I." To identify ourselves with our body or mind and yet continue to think, "This is *my* body," or "This is *my* mind," is to make nonsense out of everything. These thoughts would imply, "This is the body's body," and "This is the mind's mind," both of which are completely meaningless statements. Furthermore, there are so many atoms in our body and so many thoughts passing through our mind that if we called each one of them "I" we would have to conclude that we were a million different people. Nor is it reasonable to identify "I" with any one particular atom or thought, for then what would everything left over be? To whom would they belong?

If we think about these points systematically and use them to investigate the way in which we view ourselves, we shall come to see that there can be no such thing as an independently existing "I." The non-existence or lack of such a false "I" is what is meant by emptiness. Because ignorance believes that we exist somehow as a truly independent "I" and the wisdom of emptiness sees clearly that such an "I" has never had even the slightest existence, these two views are said to be complete opposites. Despite

what we instinctively believe about our false "I," our conventionally real "I" is neither separate from our body and mind nor is it
one with any part of them. Rather, it exists *in dependence upon*
them both.

There are the relative or conventional and the ultimate or absolute levels of truth. The conventional "I" appears to an ignorant
mind as if it were the previously mentioned false "I," that is to say
independent and self-existing, and thus is a relative truth. The
ultimate truth of this conventional "I" is the actual way in which
it exists, and this cannot be perceived by such an ignorant mind.
Only a mind that understands emptiness and realizes directly that
all things lack true independent self-existence can perceive this
absolute true nature. Such a supreme mind is unpolluted with
misconceptions concerning relative truths and thus can see things
the way they actually exist on both levels.

When we develop an insight into emptiness we shall view things
quite differently from the way we do now. It will be *as if* everything were a phantom or mirage. But this does *not* imply that
nothing exists. It is important to realize that while the "I" is
neither *separate from* nor *exactly the same* as the body and mind,
this does *not* mean it is totally non-existent. This would be a
wrong and very dangerous conclusion to draw. A person suffering
from the ordinary delusion of I-consciousness may start investigating to see what his troublesome "I" is like. After searching
and being unable to find the independent type of "I" he was
looking for, he may conclude that his "I" is totally non-existent.
Once his belief in reality has been undermined in this way, it
would not be difficult for him to deny everything. He would not
only think that in some way he himself were non-existent, but
would also harbour the same feelings about other people and
things.

This extreme view of denial, called nihilism, can lead to very
serious states of mental illness and thus to very severe suffering.
Therefore, any investigation we do of the "I" should be entered
into very carefully. We must be able to distinguish between two
completely different conceptions of "I." The ordinary mistaken
one views it as something having independent existence. When

this false view of "I" is refuted, what we are left with is the real, conventionally existing "I." This is the "I" that exists *in dependence upon* our body and mind. It performs actions, creates karma and experiences its results according to the law of cause and effect as described by the twelve links. Such an "I," because it is *not* something truly independent, is part of a long continuum of actions and reactions. As we come to understand this, we shall see that there is a reason why we experience what we do. We shall also realize how it is possible to shape our future experiences by what we think, say and do now. Thus as our wisdom grows, so will our control over our destiny.

If we make a clear distinction between the false, independent "I" and the one that actually exists, we shall not be in danger of falling into the extreme of nihilism. Otherwise, the meditation we do on emptiness will only serve to double our ignorance.

As we meditate on emptiness, we pass through several stages of insight. First we gain a clear view of how we conceive of our false "I," the one that appears to exist independently. Then, as we try to pinpoint this false "I" by checking to see if it is one with or separate from our body and mind, our "false view is dissolved" as Je Tsong-khapa has said. This "I" begins to fade and eventually disappears, dissolving into its absolute true nature.

When we can no longer find this "I," we shall experience a profoundly empty feeling within. It is as if we had lost something precious. At this point, fear may arise because we no longer have this "I" to hold onto. When and if this happens, we must be on guard not to fall into the extreme of nihilistically denying everything. This is a dangerous mistake, as mentioned before. Rather, we should persevere in our meditation and eventually a very subtle realization of emptiness will arise. We shall be able to discern the absolute true nature of the "I"—its lack of independent existence—and yet fully appreciate that it has a phantom-like existence on the relative level of truth. As stated in *Guru Puja:*

> Not even an atom of samsara or nirvana
> Has any such thing as inherent existence,
> Yet there is no fraud in saying that all of these atoms

Are dependent arisings from cause and effect.
Please bless me to realize Nagarjuna's great view
Of the non-contradictory, mutually beneficial function of
the two levels of truth.

When we gain this dual realization, we are truly on "the path that pleases the buddhas."

The mistaken way we view the "I" as something independent and self-existing is the same way we view all other phenomena. For example, when we see something such as a table, we pay no attention to the fact that it exists for us in terms of the name we call it and that this name, or label, is given to an aggregate depending upon parts, causes and circumstances. Instead of viewing the table in terms of the interdependence of all these many factors, we see it in a very simplistic and misleading way. With an instinctive wrong belief that is deeply entrenched within our mind, we feel that this object is something very real and self-sufficient, coming forward to us from the outside. We do not think of it as something we have named and, to this extent, have in fact created.

For instance, let us say that a couple has a baby and decides to call him Gerald. Despite the fact that they were the ones who created this name for him, they soon come to think of their baby as a real "Gerald." They see Gerald as something existing from the baby's side alone, independent and self-existing, appearing to them as if from without. Instead of seeing him as someone depending upon a body, mind, name and such things, they see him as a real, independent Gerald who does not depend on anything else for his existence.

There are many books telling us how to meditate further on the lack of independent self-existence of the "I" and all other phenomena. By reading such texts on emptiness we can amass a great deal of intellectual knowledge. But the most important thing is actually to purify ourselves of all wrong views, delusions and misconceptions. As long as we remain ignorant of what is proper and improper, failing to realize how distorted our picture of reality is, all our knowledge will be empty of real meaning and value. Thus, there is much purification to be done on our minds.

We must try to diminish both the gross delusions such as hatred and attachment which make it difficult for us to concentrate and penetrate into the meaning of emptiness, as well as the more subtle and fundamental one of ignorance, from which these grosser delusions arise. Furthermore, we must never neglect to observe our karma, for the strict direction of our actions is the prime dharma practice.

Eventually we shall come to see how this persistent belief in true independent existence infects the minds of all ordinary beings. Events in the marketplace and elsewhere will seem like an absurd drama in which everyone shares a common delusion. Although tragic, it makes us laugh. The process of purifying our own mind of this delusion may take a long time to complete, but it is essential if we are to escape from suffering and show others the way to freedom. Therefore, we should try our hardest, always keeping our motivation as pure as possible.

Conclusion

There has not been enough time to go into an exhaustive discussion of the three principal aspects of the path to enlightenment. But now that we have some idea why it is important to develop a full renounced mind, an enlightened motive of bodhicitta and a correct view of emptiness, we should make an effort to pursue these teachings to the best of our ability. We should try to find a spiritual master who can lead us onto a correct path of understanding. Furthermore, we must read and study valid explanations of these essential dharma points. But most importantly, we should try to tame our mind by meditating conscientiously on everything we have learned. Let us truly integrate these teachings into our daily life. In this way our practice will be pleasing to all enlightened beings and will eventually enable us to be of great benefit to others.

When we begin a meditation session on any of these teachings —in fact, whenever we are about to engage in any virtuous activity at all—we should remember to purify our motivation. This will ensure that the greatest possible benefit will follow from whatever we do. Thus please cultivate such thoughts as the following:

I, and all living beings as well, have been suffering in samsara from beginningless time up until now. And still I continue to suffer, blindly accepting as true my ignorant concept of who I am. I wrongly believe "I" to be something self-existent and, as a consequence, see the impurities of samsara as pure and desirable.

But I need not labour under these delusions any longer. There was a time before his enlightenment when Shakyamuni Buddha himself was as ignorant and deluded as I, yet eventually he was able to attain the full awakening of buddhahood. There is no reason why I cannot do likewise.

However, it is not enough that I penetrate through to reality and win liberation for myself alone. I am not the only being who desires happiness and release from pain. It is not right that I should cherish myself more than I do others. Indeed, my self-cherishing attitude has been the very source of my suffering for all these many lifetimes and therefore must be abandoned now. All living beings, these precious mothers of mine, have provided me with whatever enjoyment and happiness I have ever had. Although none of these benefactors desire to be miserable, they ignorantly destroy their chances for happiness. How can I abandon them when they are in such dire need of guidance?

My fellow humans are not the only beings who inflict punishment on themselves. Animals and all the seen and unseen creatures of the universe act in a similarly deluded manner. They have suffered from beginningless time and will continue to do so as long as they remain shrouded in ignorance. I cannot forget that all these unfortunate creatures as well have shown me great kindness.

Therefore, as I recognize my responsibility to ensure the welfare of all living beings, I shall now meditate on the profound path to enlightenment. May whatever merit generated from such activity result in the taming of my mind. May I progress through all the stages of spiritual development as quickly as possible and attain full enlightenment for the benefit of all my many mothers. May the enlightened beings' teachings of truth continue to flourish and provide comfort for all.

Thank you very much.

7 Integrating Dharma into Everyday Life

I think you have already heard enough information about dharma wisdom-knowledge. Lama Zopa has briefly outlined and explained how to actualize this knowledge and I am sure you all appreciate how effective that can be. Since you now have a good intellectual idea how to find solutions for your problems by following the dharma, I am not going to re-emphasize these points.

However, we can take a closer look at what Lama Zopa has pointed out. For instance, when he and others talk about buddha, dharma and sangha, these should not be thought of as things that have already passed. They are not subjects of mere historical interest. Nor do lamas talk merely about the future saying, "If you do such-and-such a dharma practice now, you will gain this realization in the future and it will make you happy." Lamas talk mainly about the *present*, what is happening in your mind right now.

Even when we speak about karma, the workings of cause and

effect, we are not primarily interested in demonstrating how something done last year has led to a specific experience today. Rather, we show that if you act this morning with a certain cloudy motivation, a negative effect is felt within you even on the same day. It is far more relevant to learn about such immediate changes than to gather mere historical or philosophical knowledge about remote events.

For example, Lama Zopa has talked about the three principal aspects of the path. What you learned from these lectures depends not only on what he explained, but on what was happening within you as you listened. If you paid attention in too intellectual a fashion you might have perceived that the lama had given certain teachings, but this is all you would have seen. Westerners often have the attitude, "Wow, he is really giving a fantastic talk!" But if you realize what is happening you will see that the lama is not giving out great wisdom. He is merely describing what is happening within *you,* in your mind. His only interest is to encourage you to look at yourself more closely. What he says is simple and straightforward; it is what you yourself realize as a result that makes it truly fantasitic.

Thus, so much depends on how you listen. It should be like watching an exciting movie on television. You look at it intently, anxious to know what is going to happen next. In the same way, when a lama speaks you should be attentive to see what he stirs up within you. His words and your realizations should be simultaneous. After all, dharma wisdom is not dealing with something foreign and exotic like Mount Everest. It is talking about you, only you. And it is not concerned with your body, nose or hair, but only with the state of your mind. It is interested primarily in your psychological make-up, your mental attitudes.

People may think that dharma is strictly an Eastern cultural phenomenon, but this is not so. What do we normally mean when we speak about "culture"? It is really only the relative mind, the shared illusions of a particular country or people and as such has nothing at all to do with the wisdom-truth of dharma. If we stretch the meaning of the term a little, we can say that dharma is the "culture" of our own evolutionary wisdom-knowledge. But this is not how the word is usually used.

When someone says that dharma is culturally limited, he or she is often doing so merely as an excuse. He says, "The lama is teaching about his own culture. But since it is foreign to me, I as an American cannot practise it." The mind comes up with such alibis all the time. Just observe what happens on days when you seem unable to see anything clearly. Instead of searching for the source of your confusion, you think, "O, I cannot possibly do any dharma practice today." This is a common reaction, isn't it? But it shows that there is no understanding of what dharma really means. Similarly, it is just a rationalization to think that you cannot follow the dharma when you are in the United States.

Dharma wisdom is nobody's culture. It is not America's and never will become so. Nor is it the samsaric Tibetan culture either. This is not what we are teaching. Both the Tibetan and the American cultures are samsaric, so we are certainly not interested in showing you how to exchange one for the other. The dharma teaches ways to gain inner understanding beneath the superficial level of any one nation's illusions.

What is America's culture? In the morning you get up and your mind immediately goes into the kitchen. The first thing you think about is, "Where is my coffee?" Then at lunchtime you want a hamburger. These are the things that make up America's culture, aren't they? But such samsaric culture obviously has nothing to do with dharma wisdom-knowledge. Dharma is not tied up with such external habits of a society.

How do you start the day with dharma wisdom? Instead of following your ego's instinctive call for coffee, you wake up carefully, alert to your internal feelings and state of mind. Then you establish the motivation that will take you through the rest of the day. "What is the purpose of being alive today? It must be something more important than drinking coffee. To live merely a coffee existence is not worthwhile. It is far better to dedicate this day to the development of bodhicitta, leading to the peaceful path of liberation and full awakening for the benefit of all motherly beings." Then you make the strong determination, "From this moment on, until I go to sleep, I shall stay aware of every action of my body, speech and mind. In this way I shall maintain control, placing myself in a peaceful internal environment."

If you establish this kind of mind in the morning, you will not have to keep reminding yourself of your motivation throughout the day. It will not be necessary to think, "I am trying to be a religious person; therefore I must be good." With a true motivation and a great determination established in the morning, the rest of the day will go by peacefully. Even if you encounter an angry person who shouts at you, you will remain controlled. This does not mean that you squeeze yourself, suppressing your hatred forcefully. Your self-control will be natural and calm, coming from a deep recognition of the deluded source and the disadvantages of negativities.

But do not believe this merely because I or anyone else says so. Investigate this yourself to see how thoughts and feelings come into your heart. If you do this every day, I am sure you will find the method of dharma control to be very practical.

A powerful technique for the control of the inner and outer environment involves the use of mantras. One that we often repeat is that of Shakyamuni Buddha, *om muni muni mahamuniye svaha*. Mantras are effective because they help keep your mind quiet and peaceful, automatically integrating it into one-pointedness. They make your mind receptive to very subtle vibrations and thereby heighten your perception. Their recitation eradicates gross negativities and the true nature of things can then be reflected in your mind's resulting clarity. By practising a transcendental mantra, you can in fact purify all the defiled energy of your body, speech and mind.

Whether repetition of a mantra is a transcendental meditation or not depends on you and your wisdom. Its power does not come solely from itself. It is not as if there were some ancient sacred syllables that you could recite without contemplation and they would bring you great spiritual benefit automatically. This is a misconception. For instance, if you are under the sway of craving desire, your mindless recitation of the most blessed mantra in the universe will be of limited benefit. It will be just another samsaric activity.

Suppose you are sitting somewhere reciting a mantra yet thinking, "chocolate, chocolate, delicious chocolate." If you are totally preoccupied by the thought of this or some other super-market treat, how can such a practice ever be a transcendental meditation? How can it lead to an everlasting peaceful result? For a mantra to be effective you need to have stilled your mind to a certain extent and to have gained at least some measure of con-centration.

In addition, you should have a pure motivation. It is not enough to be concerned with gaining temporal pleasure for yourself. The true purpose of mantras, as with all other dharma practices, is to benefit all motherly sentient beings. Rather than always thinking, "I want, I want," try to develop the pure wish to be helpful to others. You need not be either too intellectual or super-emotional about this. Merely dedicate the mantra's energy for this altruistic purpose and beneficial results will follow by themselves.

Mantras also have the power to cure diseases. For example, sometimes people become temporarily insane because they are preoccupied with the false energy of their distorted minds. The purifying vibration of a mantra is able to bring the mind back to a calm and smoothly functioning state and the mental illness is thereby cured. Since physical diseases are also intimately related to distorted states of mind, mantras are effective as part of their treatment as well. There is nothing magical about this. Scientific experimentation has clearly demonstrated their healing powers.

The specific connotation of the Buddha mantra, *om muni muni mahamuniye svaha,* is "control, control, greatest control." Now you might think that Buddhism emphasizes control too much and feel that the lamas are saying, "Your deluded mind is so full of negativities that you must restrict it tightly." But this is not what we mean. Rather, if in the morning you establish a certain kind of mind, you will automatically be more conscious of your actions during the day. Once set, your mind's internal watch continues to run by itself. This is true because by channelling a great deal of energy in one direction you ensure that all subsequent energy will flow along the same path.

In Tibet we say that directing the mind is "like bridling a fine horse to make him rideable." A horse is a tremendously powerful animal and if you do not have the means to control him properly he may gallop off wildly, possibly destroying himself and others as well. If you can harness all that energy, however, the horse's great strength can be used for accomplishing many difficult tasks. The same applies to yourself. Looked at scientifically, your body, speech and mind are nothing but varying forms of energy. Thus, if in the morning you direct this energy by strongly affirming your motivation, all the remaining energy of body, speech and mind will follow in the same direction. So the control we are talking about is similar to that of a pilot who does not *restrict* but rather *directs* the power of his aeroplane. The problem with language is that words cannot really describe inner experiences exactly. But if you yourself practise a particular teaching and gain a realization from it, then such words as "control" will no longer be any problem for you.

The most important part of the day is the morning. Perhaps sometimes when you wake up you have a headache or your leg hurts. But the first thing you should do, instead of becoming involved in this pain, is make a strong determination as to what attitude you are going to maintain for the rest of the day by cultivating the pure motivation of bodhicitta. If you decide to do this practice, the first day might prove a little difficult. But each day after that it will become easier and easier to cultivate this pure motivation. This will be the result of developing and conditioning your mind in a particular virtuous direction.

No matter how much most of us read about dharma, we rarely devote even one day to experimenting with such a practice. But if you were to try, eventually your mind would become the embodiment of peaceful awareness. Of course, when you begin any such spiritual practice of mental training, you are only imitating something you have heard. This is to be expected at the initial stages of any practice. If you do not realize this, however, you might easily lose patience with what you are doing and think it forced and unnatural. You may be sitting in meditation posture someday expecting a miracle, and when it does not happen you may ask yourself, "Why am I following this strange Eastern custom?" Then the negative mind will answer, "You are just aping that foreign lama's way of sitting. There is no good reason to do so. Why don't you sit in a comfortable chair like other Americans?"

Thus you have to be very careful with the mind. It knows very well how to rationalize why you should not follow methods intended to tame it. You should know enough to disregard the scepticism of this doubting mind and continue your practices steadily and patiently.

Another thing to realize is that there are often two types of mind working within you at the same time. For instance, while you are sweeping your room, one of these minds is paying attention to what you are doing on the physical level, while the other may be concentrating on a mantra. This does not mean that these two minds are in conflict or that your repetition of the mantra is insincere. Even while practising dharma, you are still involved in the relative and mundane aspects of life. To live, there are many things you simply must do, such as work to earn money, make tea and coffee, prepare food and so forth. These are not activities you should try to avoid. Merely realize that they make up only the relative level of your existence. Thus, while the mind engaged in worldly affairs is sweeping your room, simultaneously the wisdom mind can be functioning.

Sometimes the method for directing this functioning is a mantra. A mantra is energy, but not at all involved with ordinary vibrations. Rather it is absolutely pure, created by simple wisdom-knowledge. Thus if your mind is generating such pure wisdom-energy, you can be the embodiment of peace even while performing relatively mundane actions. In this respect the mind is very much like an ocean which basically has a calm nature even while there are violent waves on its surface.

If you are tuned into wisdom-knowledge, you can transform the energy of your relative environment—colours, sensations and the like—into bliss. Thus the external energy of what you perceive will not be able to grab hold of your mind, arousing desire, attraction and other negativities. Rather, your mind can control and transmute this environment into something transcendent. With this kind of direction or control, you do not interpret different phenomena in terms of attachment. Thus all the other related delusions will not arise either. You are not tossed up and down involuntarily by the various good and bad things that happen to you.

At this point there may be the nagging question, "If you transcend such environmental objects and transform them into something else, are you not merely creating mental projections? How can a method that denies reality ever be effective?" Westerners are generally very intelligent and such a question can easily arise. But in answer let me ask another question: "Is there anything you see that is really 'good' or 'bad'?" You may *think* that something you see as good or bad really exists that way, but how do you *know* this is so? I do not think you can come up with a satisfactory answer to that question. You may say, "Because I feel it to be true." But why do you feel that way? "Because I saw it with my eyes." But then the question is, "Is what your eyes tell you always correct? Do you always see reality free from obscuring mental projections?" "No, of course not," you will answer, "but *this* time what I saw was real." How do you know? I can guarantee that there is absolutely no definitive answer to that question. You may think about it for a lifetime but it will be difficult to come up with an answer that will be totally satisfying.

Do not miss the point of all this. This question is not difficult because it is some sort of obscure philosophical point. It is not merely a theoretical problem. It comes out of your own experience. The problem is that you are not seeing the absolute true nature of any phenomenon. Without perceiving this, it is very difficult to talk about reality. When I ask, "How do you know whether what you see is real or not?" do not think, "Wow, he is giving me a tough question. I think only the lama himself knows the answer to that one." It is not like that at all. No one is hiding a profound answer from you. You will only begin to make sense out of this problem when you investigate your own experiences of what you call "reality."

Consider what often happens in the United States when a black and a white person confront one another. They do not really see each other at all. Rather, the white paints a threatening black visualization and vice versa. Then, on the basis of this, they act towards each other in certain definite and predetermined ways. Why do these different discriminations have the power to influence their minds? After all, they are only mental projections having nothing whatsoever to do with the reality of each other's character. It is not *what* they see but the *way* they see that makes all the difference. This is visualization. Furthermore, what they visualize is not something that a lama taught them; it is part of their own culture. Thus when I talk of transcending the relative reality of anything by constructing the proper visualization, I am not talking about something that is alien to what people do all the time anyway. It is something that strongly influences the mind and, when purified by the proper motivation, can be extremely beneficial.

You know by experience that when you let sunlight into a darkened room, the darkness disappears immediately. There is no question about this, is there? The same thing happens when you visualize Shakyamuni Buddha, the reflection of radiant sun-like wisdom. The effect is automatic, bestowing blessings on your mind and leading to control. When your visualization of him is strong and clear—and you recognize that his body is not made up of substantial physical energy but is solely the manifestation of the dharmakaya, true wisdom-knowledge—then even five or ten minutes of such a visualization is tremendously effective. You do not need words; the visualization itself is enough.

Let us say you are walking down a New York City street and you see some beautiful clothing in a shop window that stirs up grasping desire and other conflicting emotions in your mind. Right then and there you can transmute that energy into the radiant wisdom form of Buddha; or, if you know how, you can even dissolve that energy into its void nature. When by these methods you realize that the grasping attitude you have projected onto this piece of clothing exists only for a deluded relative mind and therefore has nothing whatsoever to do with reality, then whatever delusions have been aroused will automatically disappear. All difficulties will vanish. Otherwise, if your mind remains tied to your deluded mental projection and you think, "Oh, it is so beautiful, I wish it were mine," you might carry this alluring image around with you all day.

If you stop and think, you will see that this is really what happens. You might feel, "The lama talks a lot, but what he says is just speculation. It has no basis in fact." However, you should not reject or accept any teachings blindly. Rather, experiment with them and see for yourself whether they are true or not. As I have said before, dharma is not so much concerned with the past and the future as it is with the very present. So try these teachings out yourself and see if they are worthwhile.

Another doubt may arise at this point. You may think, "I can use this method of transformation for dealing with beautiful and attractive objects easily enough. But what about when a tremendous problem arises? Perhaps someone gives me a hard time or even beats me. How do I control that?" This is an important consideration. Yet, if you are sufficiently aware and mindful, even these unpleasant situations can be transformed into a dharma practice.

The first thing to do when involved in a painful relationship with someone or something is to remember that reacting negatively never helps at all. Feeling sorry for yourself, acting defensively and expressing hostility accomplish nothing. They only make you even more nervous and upset. Thinking dispassionately about your past experiences will convince you this is true. As negative thoughts and feeings lead only to immediate and future suffering, it is important to adopt a more beneficial way of reacting.

Thus, instead of giving in to sorrow and hatred, look closely at what is happening within and without you and caution yourself, "Wait a moment. Calm down. This too will pass." If you can hold off expressing your anger for even a few seconds, your mind will clear a little by itself. In this more reasonable state you can approach the situation much more skilfully.

Remember that there must be a cause for what is happening to you now. Perhaps you are reaping the karmic fruit of your aggressive actions towards others in the past. Thus you can be relieved that you are repaying your debt so lightly. If this encounter causes you much suffering, you can still consider it a blessing. "Maybe whoever or whatever is bothering me is really a manifestation of an enlightened being's dharma wisdom, assuming this form to grant me realizations. If I can learn from this pain to be more compassionate towards those who are suffering and to avoid actions that bring such suffering on myself, then it is worthwhile for someone to give me a bad time. If everyone treated me like a baby, I would never have the chance to mature emotionally or spiritually." With such thoughts it is possible to exchange your hatred for gratitude and to do so sincerely with deep understanding.

It is true that this is an unaccustomed way of handling adverse circumstances and it might sound rather naive or even crazy to most ordinary people. But to someone possessing dharma wisdom-knowledge, this an excellent path to real growth. He or she sees that the usual and conventionally acceptable way of reacting to problems is deluded, leading to more and more pain and discomfort for everyone. Taking advantage of all harmful situations to learn something profound about one's own mind, however, is extremely beneficial.

It is impossible to exist without continually relating to other people, especially in a big city. Certainly some of these relationships are bound to be annoying. But as long as we have to continue communicating with other people, we might as well learn as much as possible in the process. After all, we are not yet perfect. There is still a great deal more maturing to do and understanding to acquire.

All this holds true especially for couples and others living in very close, continual contact. As such people are bound to clash with each other occasionally, there must be a lot of understanding to help sustain the relationship. Even if one of them behaves badly on purpose, there will be no problem if the other has sincerely internalized dharma wisdom-knowledge. Negativities can even become occasions for mutual benefit if they can be transformed into dharma.

Although there is great value in kindness, you do not always learn by being sweet to everyone and saying, "I love you. I'll be good to you." Perhaps you are acting in this way because you want favours, protection or security in return. If you make yourself dependent on others in this way, you will never discover and develop your own abilities. Do not think that you lack strength. It is the characteristic of the human mind that it possesses incredible power. All you have to do is manifest it through your actions. Instead of interpeting situations in such a way that you become depressed, you should make use of them to increase your wisdom. In this way you can transmute even unpleasant conditions into the everlasting peaceful path of liberation. In the Tibetan texts that discuss the training of the mind, this is known as "changing adverse circumstances into a path to enlightenment."

Often when encountering something unpleasant, people say, "How terrible!" If you probe deeply, asking again and again what is so horribly wrong with the situation, there is no satisfactory answer that can finally be given. No one can prove that anything is inherently "terrible." Thus whatever ordinary minds find distasteful can be transformed by the dharma wisdom-knowledge into an effective spiritual path. This is definitely possible and something that all of us, especially in a big city, need very badly.

Westerners have a special advantage when listening to such teachings on transforming bad circumstances into good. In other less scientific cultures it might be difficult to understand how things can be transmuted from one thing to another. But in your educational system there is much emphasis on studying the various cycles of change found in the external environment. Thus when you hear about ways to transmute internal mental states and thus affect your emotional life, you can understand at least intellectually how this might be possible.

Most people in America work for someone else. This provides many opportunities for taking advantage of what otherwise might be difficult or boring situations. In the morning before going to work, you should reaffirm your motivation. Remembering the pervasive nature of suffering, you should generate compassionate thoughts for all your fellow beings. Then you should dedicate the day's energy for the benefit of others. You should see your job as a particular commitment of that energy and thus determine to perform it as diligently as possible. With such a stable foundation, you will not fall prey to laziness, boredom or resentment when you arrive at work. Realizing that there is no advantage, financial or otherwise, in cheating your boss by working inefficiently, you can proceed with your tasks in a way pleasing to both him and to yourself. With such an attitude, your day can prove very worthwhile and purposeful instead of being a meaningless waste of time.

Many people nowadays are very interested in various forms of physical discipline. These activities, designed to increase control over the body, can be very beneficial. But working to control your mind and thereby benefit others is an exercise of even greater value. By means of such mental discipline you can achieve outstanding results, including the attainment of full enlightenment. One of the most effective ways of applying this discipline is to transform all ordinary situations into a spiritual path.

In the time of Shakyamuni Buddha, there was an old man who wanted very much to follow the dharma. Unfortunately he was very dull-witted and found it impossible to understand even one verse of Buddha's teachings. The disciples of Shakyamuni were so discouraged by this man's inability to learn anything that they felt it was hopeless to try to teach him. Thus, after being rejected by one monk after another, this saddened old man felt there was nothing left to do but throw himself in the river and end his pitiful existence.

With his unsurpassable insight, Shakyamuni Buddha saw what was about to happen and immediately sent one of his closest followers to dissuade the man and tell him that Buddha himself would give him a spiritual practice. When the despondent man was brought before him, Buddha said kindly, "It is not necessary that you receive detailed teachings, say prayers or repeat verses. Your practice will be to sweep out the temple and keep it as tidy as possible. As you brush out the dirt, however, think to yourself, 'Be rid of this dirt! Remove this bad smell!' It will be sufficient for you to do this much."

Encouraged that he now had a practice that was simple enough to follow, the old man began his task enthusiastically. Each day he would clean the temple, repeating the simple instructions he had received. Then one day, as he was sweeping the dust from the temple floor as usual, he began to think, "I feel I understand now what 'Be rid of this dirt!' really means. The dirt is not outside; it is inside. And the bad smell is not here in the temple; it too is within me. It is not the temple I should clean, but my own mind." Bang! This sudden insight shot through his delusions with such force that he immediately gained a deep realization of the four noble truths, the profound essence of the entire path. Thus in a split second he was transformed from an ignorant sweeper into a noble one, a glorious arya being.

As this story illustrates, you do not have to receive a great deal of detailed information to develop the wisdom-knowledge of the dharma. What is necessary is that everything you learn and experience goes directly into your heart and appears immediately in your actions. In this way, even if you hear only a few teachings, they can open your mind completely. It is not *what* you learn but *how* you learn it that is of primary importance. The old man had received the briefest teachings imaginable, but as soon as he understood how they related to his life, he achieved very advanced realizations.

In a similar fashion, you should transform everything you perceive—all sights, sounds, smells and so forth—into dharma wisdom-knowledge. This is much healthier than emotionally grasping at or rejecting what you encounter. If your outlook is comprehensive enough to include everything in your internal and external environment as part of an integrated whole, your life will seem very worthwhile. Instead of seeing the world through the murkiness of hatred, attachment and ignorance, everything will appear clear and pure.

Many times the fogginess you perceive is more a part of your projection than anything to do with the object itself. For instance, it is common while walking through New York City streets to think that all the bustling activity there is polluted. But this is not necessarily true. It is because of your own insecure feelings, heightened by the rush of traffic and events, that everyone appears to be angry at everyone else. If you stop to speak with someone, however, very likely you will find that his or her heart is the same as yours. It is only a superficial judgement based on fleeting impressions that decides New York and New Yorkers are hostile.

The mind is full of many similar misconceptions. Some people may believe that since wrong views are philosophical in nature, they must be learned in order to be acquired. But this is not generally so. Misconceptions do not have to be transferred from one mind to another; nor do they necessarily depend on an elaborate line of false reasoning. Rather, the mind, thrown by karma and delusions into a contaminated body, is already steeped in many wrong views, such as believing the "I" to be an independent and self-sufficient entity. These mistaken beliefs do not depend on words or philosophical ideas. In fact, it is the other way around. It is only when a deluded mind tries to express itself on a conscious level that it uses words to convey its distorted perceptions. So do not think that your mind is free of misconceptions because you never studied philosophy at school.

Looking at the mind to discover and correct its delusions is very interesting, isn't it? If you examine things in terms of dharma wisdom-knowledge, there will never be a chance of becoming bored. It is fascinating to see how quickly the mind creates and reacts to new situations. Even more fascinating is to gain control over this process and see how easily everything can be transformed into a spiritual practice. Many people, whether they have a job or not, feel that they have nothing worthwhile to do in their lives. But dharma wisdom can keep you occupied at all times. By watching your mind, you will always be busy learning something new, and the knowledge gained will always be practical. Unlike a student who gains all his or her information from books, this knowledge grows out of your own experience of life. It is good if you can learn from both books and your experience, but clearly the latter method is far more valuable.

To be born a human is really very fortunate. As such, you have the precious ability to use your understanding with discrimination. The big difference between yourself and a dog is that you are able to examine your own behaviour while a dog cannot. Because you can judge whether or not your mental and physical actions are wholesome, you have both a great opportunity and a great responsibility to see the nature of your faults and short-comings. While this is much more difficult than noticing what is wrong with others, it is very beneficial if you can discover and root out these weaknesses in yourself. What a shame it would be not to take advantage of this rare endowment and instead follow your instincts blindly and uncritically! Thus, whether what you encounter is good or bad, you should experiment as much as possible with the purest dharma wisdom-knowledge, transforming everything into the everlasting peaceful path to enlightenment.

As indicated before, there are certain problems faced by Westerners who return from the East after having studied the dharma under a lama or guru there. Perhaps you miss the ceremonies that might have accompanied your studies and feel you cannot continue your practices effectively without them. For instance, it is very common in the East to mark a significant occasion by performing a puja. In such a ceremony, drums, cymbals and bells are often used to accompany the chanting of a particular scriptural text. This is done before an altar supporting pictures of enlightened beings and often elaborately decorated with candles, water bowls, incense, butter lamps, plates of food and sculptures. Such puja ceremonies can be very engrossing, and it is easy to feel that they are an integral and indispensible part of your dharma practice.

"Puja" is a Sanskrit word meaning "offering." Why do people give offerings to someone else? Usually it is to please the other person and make him happy. This is the lower, relative interpretation. But in terms of the dharma, "puja" has a more profound connotation. When you transform everything into beautiful sights, sounds, smells and so forth and offer them in a puja to representations of the fully enlightened omniscient mind, it is you yourself who benefits. By directing your energy through such a ceremony towards the thought of enlightenment, you bring yourself closer to achieving everlasting pleasure and peace.

Thus you have to understand what the essential element of a puja is. It is not the chanting or the piece of fruit you carefully place on the altar that is the true offering. Whatever action or meditation you do that brings your mind closer to everlasting joy, destroying confusion and agitation—*that* is the real puja. Thus, you should not think that since there are no Tibetan or Indian ceremonies to attend in America you cannot practise the dharma. You do not need the ting, ting, ting of a bell or the clash of cymbals to perform a puja. Whatever you do, even eating and drinking, can be turned into an offering. It is only a matter of keeping your motivation pure.

For instance, here in America people are always drinking something. In fact, since I arrived in New York I have not been able to stop drinking; it has been so hot! Now, whenever you are thirsty and reach for a glass of water or whatever, check up on your mind. Instead of unconsciously gulping the drink down, look inwards for a second and offer it to your attainment of full enlightenment. If you have received teachings on the blessing mantra, *om ah hum*, it is good to recite it. But even if you have not, by looking within your mind you can transform the water into the purest nectar. By directing the energy of what you are drinking towards higher selfless purposes, you automatically receive powerful blessings. This whole process of transformation takes only a few moments, yet is as effective as an elaborate puja in elevating your mind beyond its ordinary level.

The noble Nagarjuna has said that we should not use our precious human body for unworthy aims. Thus, when you nourish and take care of your physical form, do not do so out of vanity, wishing to appear attractive to others. Rather, think that you are maintaining your health and strength in order to be of the most benefit to yourself and others. It takes a great deal of energy to follow a spiritual path and attain the loftiest goals. Thus, you must transform all the energy coming into your body into the everlasting peaceful path to enlightenment.

The best way to utilize energy properly is by staying aware and

conscious of whatever happens to you. Simple acts become
dharma when performed consciously with full awareness. For
instance, when you eat or drink, be mindful of the sensations
aroused in your nervous system. When Shakyamuni Buddha was
alive, there was no such thing as an external puja. Meditation
itself was puja. In the same way, if you can remain as alert while
eating and drinking as you are in meditation, then all of your
actions will become a dharma offering.

Internal feelings and sensations are aroused whenever you do
any activity. When they come up, do not immediately think,
"This is good" or "This is bad." Such automatic reactions only
generate confusion, obscuring the reality of what is actually
happening. Instead, try to be mindful of all these feelings and
sensations and investigate them with introspective wisdom. This
will develop in you the habit of alertness, making your mind
clearer and less distracted.

In order to become fully conscious of your actions, it is necessary to regulate your behaviour to some extent. Thus when you are
eating, it is usually best not to talk too much. Simple matters may
be discussed, but save complicated subjects requiring a great deal
of thought for later. Otherwise your mind will flit from one
thought to another and, instead of concentrating on the sensation
of eating, you will be travelling around the world running into
problems and confusion. Thus, if you want a peaceful environment, it is better not to talk too much.

However, when you have finished eating and it is time for discussion, you should turn your mind to that, again with full awareness. Pay attention to what is going on, not to the meal just ended
or the next one coming up. And do not babble on senselessly,
changing topics with every sentence. This only encourages the
habit of sloppy-mindedness which is already deeply engrained.
Through innumerable past lives we have all been performing
mindless actions, heedless of the reality of the present moment.
Thus it has been impossible to grasp the whole of any situation,
for everything seems hopelessly mixed together to our unfo-
cussed mind. Thus we must train this mind, and a good way to

begin is by concentrating on what we are doing and not being distracted by extraneous thoughts or fantasies.

Your school experiences should have convinced you of the importance of a concentrated mind. If you have too many subjects to learn, it is very difficult to do well in any one of them. Your energy is spread too thin for you to gain any real understanding of what you are studying. But when you focus your attention on one subject at a time, your mind is able to receive a clear and vivid impression of it. Thus, instead of letting your mind be passively led from one thought to another, it is important to maintain control over your mental processes.

Extend this control to all your activities and consciously direct your body, speech and mind rather than lazily letting them lead you around. Be as one-pointed as possible and integrate your actions. This is very good for your mind since it reduces conflict and confusion and allows you to break out of the restricting mold of past bad habits. These habits only involve you in suffering, so it is important to combat them as much as possible by developing alertness and mindfulness.

Everything said here about waking, working, eating and drinking holds true for going to sleep as well. Most of the time, people fall asleep with their mind in an uncontrolled or even disturbed state. It is much better to maintain awareness while falling asleep than to do so distractedly. If you can meditate while in bed, this is extremely beneficial since your entire sleep can then be transformed into dharma wisdom. In the vast Mahayana teachings there are very detailed explanations on how to use the sleep and dream states to best advantage. But here it is sufficient to say that by concentrating your mind beforehand, you can assure yourself of a restful and beneficial sleep.

Many times, after a particularly stimulating day, you may think, "I just can't fall asleep. What can I do?" The mind is tossed in so many directions by the day's energy still echoing in your brain that sleep is impossible. Meditation can focus your mind when it is in such an agitated state and allow it to calm down so that you can go to sleep. Some of you already know that this is true from your own experience. Even during the day, how many times have you fallen asleep while meditating?

You should check carefully to see what mental impressions are predominant as you await sleep. You may have been very conscious of your actions throughout the day, but if you go to sleep without examining your mind, you can waste whatever positive energy you have created. The resulting pollution that might arise in your dreams will cancel your gains, and your thoughts upon awakening will be full of negativities.

One of the reasons it is necessary to go to sleep peacefully is that the dream state is much more powerful and effective than the waking one. You may not believe this and think, "During the day I can be conscious of my actions. I am open completely and can experience everything, physically as well as mentally. But at night my mind is just dreaming, creating mental projections. Therefore how can this unconscious state be the more powerful one?"

The reason I say this is that while you may think you are paying exclusive attention to something while awake, your other senses are still open and respond to the conflicting impressions they receive. During your dreams, however, the five physical senses—seeing, hearing, smelling, tasting and touching—are not active. When you see something in a dream, for instance, you do so with you mind's eye not your physical one. In the absence of such sensory distractions, then, your mind is left naturally concentrated with great energy. Thus the effect of dreaming about greed, for instance, can be much stronger and leave a deeper imprint on your mind than when a stray thought of attachment arises in your heart during the day. And, of course, the same holds true if you can focus in your dreams on an aspect of the spiritual path.

You must investigate the truth of all these statements for yourself. Do not rely on my words because they come from a lama. Experiment and see what the effect is of gaining control over your mind, both during the day and at night. If your practice is sincere, you should experience noticeable results in a very short time, so begin right now.

If you experiment with dharma wisdom-knowledge correctly, you will not have anxiety about attaining the final goal. There will be no need to cling desperately to your practices thinking, "I'll kill myself if I don't become enlightened right this instant!" Do not set a deadline for yourself; this will only lead to discouragement. Just be mindful of your actions and keep your motivation as pure as possible. In this way you will reach your goal naturally.

I am very happy to have possibly contributed a small drop to your ocean of knowledge. I hope you can all put dharma wisdom into practice in your own lives. This would be most worthwhile. Thank you. Thank you. Thank you so much.

Glossary

The page references after each item indicate either its first appearance in the text or where it is defined more extensively.

abhidharma   the Buddhist teachings dealing with philosophy and metaphysics; 7.

arhat   one who has attained complete liberation from suffering; 101.

arya   noble one; a superior being having attained bare perception of the true nature of reality; 134.

asura   anti-god; titan; a god-like being suffering from extreme jealousy; 93, 94.

Atisha   eleventh century Indian guru who travelled to Tibet, composed the prototype for future *Lam-rim* texts, and founded the Kadam tradition; 7.

bodhicitta   (pronounced: bodhichitta) 12, 101; cf. enlightened motive of bodhicitta.

bodhisattva   an enlightenment-bound being; someone who works to attain buddhahood for the sake of freeing all others from their suffering; a follower of the Mahayana path; 7, 103.

buddha   an awakened one; a fully enlightened being; one who has overcome all obstacles and completed all good qualities and is therefore able to benefit all other beings to the maximum extent;

first of the three jewels of refuge; 5, 21, 27.

buddha dharma the teachings of fully enlightened beings, specifically those of Shakyamuni Buddha; 5.

buddhahood the state of full awakening; full enlightenment; the goal of the Mahayana practitioner; 20.

Chandrakirti Indian commentator who elucidated the emptiness teachings of Nagarjuna; 112.

cause and effect the process whereby virtuous actions lead to happiness and non-virtuous ones to suffering; the law of karma; 30.

compassion the wish that all beings be separated from their suffering; 89, 104.

correct view of emptiness the view that understands the true nature of things: their emptiness of independent self-existence; third of the three principal aspects of the path to enlightenment; 83, 112.

cyclic existence 64, 82; cf. samsara.

deva a god; a being inhabiting the highest, most pleasurable realm of samsaric existence; 93.

dharma spiritual teachings, specifically those of fully enlightened beings; second of the three jewels of refuge; 5, 24, 27, 66.

dharmakaya the ominiscient wisdom and the emptiness of the mind of fully enlightened beings; 129.

dharma protector tutelary of an individual or a group practising Buddhism; 9.

ego-grasping the compulsion, arising from ignorance, to regard one's own personality or "I" as permanent, unchanging and existing self-sufficiently, independent of all other phenomena; 64.

emptiness (Sanskrit: shunyata) the actual way in which all things exist; refutation of the apparent independent self-existence of things; voidness; 83, 113, 116.

enlightened being one who has travelled a spiritual path to completion and has developed the compassion, wisdom and skilful means to lead sentient beings to liberation from suffering; a buddha; 75.

enlightened motive of bodhicitta the motivation to attain the full enlightenment of buddhahood in order to be able to benefit all sentient beings; the Mahayana motivation, that of a bodhisattva; second of the three principal aspects of the path to enlightenment; 69, 83, 101.

enlightenment   20; cf. buddhahood.

equilibrium   the state of mind in which one sees no essential difference between friend, enemy and stranger; equanimity; a prerequisite for the successful development of bodhicitta; 103.

four noble truths   (more accurately, the four truths of the noble ones) the theme of Shakyamuni Buddha's teachings as presented in his first discourse; the noble truths of suffering, the cause of suffering, the cessation of suffering, and the path to the cessation of suffering; 134.

full awakening   76, 123; cf. buddhahood.

full enlightenment   20, 31; cf. buddhahood.

fully renounced mind   the attitude with which one turns away from suffering, its causes and repeated, involuntary rebirth in samsara; first of the three principal aspects of the path to enlightenment; 83.

geshe   a title indicating completion and mastery of the traditional Buddhist monastic education; 6.

gompa   monastery; convent; secluded residence of religious practitioners; 5.

graded course to enlightenment   organization of the buddha dharma into stages for the orderly training of a disciple's mind; lam-rim; 6.

guru   spiritual guide and teacher; 5, 68.

Guru Shakyamuni Buddha   76; cf. Shakyamuni Buddha.

Heruka Chakrasamvara   tantric meditational deity of the compassion family; 7, 83.

incarnate lama   a highly-realized being who takes voluntary rebirth in order to continue teaching the dharma; tulku; 8; cf. rinpoche.

initiation   empowerment allowing one to receive and practise tantric teachings; 6.

Je Tsong-khapa   fifteenth century reformer of Buddhism in Tibet; author of extensive sutra and tantra teachings, most importantly the *Lam-rim chen-mo* and *Ngag-rim chen-mo;* 6, 80, 113.

karma that which brings about action and its result; the workings of cause and effect; 30, 32.

Kyabje Phabongkha Rinpoche root guru of the Senior and Junior Tutors to His Holiness the Fourteenth Dalai Lama; 83.

lama spiritual guide and teacher; guru; 5.

lam-rim stages of the path; a text outlining the graded course to enlightenment; 6.

liberation freedom from the sufferings of samsara; the state attained by an arhat; 20, 82.

lightning vehicle tantric teachings capable of bringing one to full enlightenment in one lifetime; tantrayana; vajrayana; 103.

love the wish that all beings be happy; 104.

Madhyamika the middle way philosophy as expounded by Nagarjuna elucidating the emptiness-teachings of Buddha; 7.

Mahayana the great vehicle; the path of the bodhisattva on his or her way to the full enlightenment of buddhahood; 5, 33.

mantra words of power; syllables, generally Sanskrit, recited during certain meditational practices; 30, 124.

Marpa guru of Milarepa and disciple of Naropa; 9.

meditation the process of becoming deeply acquainted with virtuous states of mind; 8, 16, 18, 44.

meditational deity a visualized figure, used in meditation, representing a specific aspect of the full enlightenment of buddhahood; 7, 83.

Milarepa eleventh century Tibetan poet and meditator famous for his intense guru-devotion; 9, 84.

Nagarjuna great second century Indian expounder of Madhyamika philosophy; chief propagator of Buddha's wisdom-teachings on emptiness; 97, 112.

narak the lowest realm of existence filled with hellish suffering; 89, 90.

Naropa Indian yogi, guru of Marpa; 6.

nihilism the extreme of denial; the mistaken and dangerous view that confuses emptiness with nothingness and leads to denial of the law of cause and effect; 117.

nirvana the state beyond sorrow; freedom from karma, delusion and repeated rebirth in samsara; 20.

pandit   master of the Buddhist arts and sciences; 112.

Prajnaparamita   the perfection of wisdom; teachings of Shakyamuni Buddha concerning emptiness in the context of the enlightened motive of bodhicitta; 7.

preta   hungry ghost; an intensely suffering being plagued by hunger and thirst; 89, 92.

puja   offering; offering ceremony; 136.

pure land   a state of existence outside samsara where all conditions are favourable for becoming fully enlightened; buddha-field; 100.

rinpoche   precious one; Tibetan title accorded to incarnate lamas and others; 5, 25.

samsara   the vicious circle of death and rebirth, fraught with suffering, which is born from ignorance of the true nature of reality; 62, 87.

sangha   monastic community following the dharma; more specifically, the assembly of arya beings on the path to liberation and full enlightenment; third of the three jewels of refuge; 10, 27.

Sera   one of the three large monastic centres located in the vicinity of Lhasa, Tibet, Sera Je being one of its two colleges; 6.

Shakyamuni Buddha   Sage of the Shakya Clan; Gautama Buddha; the fourth of the thousand buddhas of this present aeon; expounder of the dharma in India during the sixth century B.C.; 32.

Shantideva   buddhist scholar and poet of the seventh century; 7, 89.

shunyata   cf. emptiness.

stupa   monument housing a relic and symbolizing the divine mind of enlightened beings; 10.

sutra   discourse of Shakyamuni Buddha; the pre-tantric course of study in Buddhism; 6.

tantra   advanced teachings of Shakyamuni Buddha leading to the speedy attainment of full enlightenment; 6, 69, 103; cf. lightning vehicle.

three jewels of refuge   buddha, dharma and sangha; the triple gem; 75.

three principal aspects of the path to enlightenment the three-fold theme of the buddha dharma: the fully renounced mind, the enlightened motive of bodhicitta and the correct view of emptiness; 74, 83.

traditions of Buddhism unbroken teaching lineages preserving the insights of the buddha dharma; the most notable of the intertwined Tibetan traditions are the Nyingma, the no longer separately existing Kadam, the Kagyü, Sakya and Gelug; 5, 8, 12.

triple gem 27; cf. three jewels of refuge.

vinaya rules of discipline and the teachings on the law of cause and effect.

voidness cf. emptiness.

wisdom-knowledge deep understanding of the true nature of reality allowing one to deal effectively with the conventional appearance of things; 25, 35.

yogi one who follows the yoga discipline of a tantric spiritual path leading to enlightenment; 20, 80.

Suggested Further Reading

Amipa, Lama Sherab Gyaltsen. *The Opening of the Lotus*. Boston: Wisdom, 1987. Basic teachings from the Sakya tradition of Tibetan Buddhism in a clear and contemporary style.

Batchelor, Stephen. *The Jewel in the Lotus*. Boston: Wisdom, 1987. An excellent introduction to Tibetan Buddhism, containing selected teachings from the Nyingma, Kadam, Kagyu, Sakya and Geluk traditions.

Dhargyey, Geshe Ngawang. *An Anthology of Well-Spoken Advice*. Volume 1. Dharamsala: Library of Tibetan Works and Archives, 1982. A superbly detailed volume based on the great Lam-rim texts of Je Tsong Khapa and Pabongka Rinpoche.

Evans-Wentz, W.Y. *Tibet's Great Yogi Milarepa*. Oxford: Oxford University Press, 1928, 1969. This famous biography of Tibet's most revered poet-saint is an absorbing account of the spiritual quest and intense guru-devotion.

Guenther, Herbert (trans). *The Jewel Ornament of Liberation*.

Boston: Shambhala, 1959, 1971. Milarepa's disciple Gampopa combines Kadam teachings on the graded path to enlightenment with the profound mahamudra lineage of Tilopa and Naropa.

Gyatso, Tenzin, His Holiness the Fourteenth Dalai Lama. *The Buddhism of Tibet*. Ithaca: Snow Lion, 1976. Combined volume including the Dalai Lama's *Buddhism of Tibet and Key to the Middle Way,* Nagarjuna's *The Precious Garland* and the Seventh Dalai Lama's *The Song of the Four Mindfulnesses.*

—. *Kindness, Clarity and Insight*. Ithaca: Snow Lion, 1988. A marvelous collection of public talks by the present Dalai Lama on a wide range of topics as well as on many aspects of Buddhism and its application to modern life.

—. *The Meaning of Life from a Buddhist Perspective*. Boston: Wisdom, 1992. A clear explanation by His Holiness of the twelve links of independent origination translated and edited by Jeffrey Hopkins.

—. *Opening the Eye of New Awareness*. Boston: Wisdom, 1991. A succinct yet thorough presentation of Buddhist teachings.

Kunga, Lama and Brian Cutillo. *Drinking the Mountain Stream*. Novato, CA: Lotsawa, 1978. Lama Kunga Rinpoche, a highly respected master of the Sakya tradition and an incarnation of one of Milarepa's closest disciples, presents stories and songs newly translated from a rare collection of Milarepa's work.

Longchenpa. *Kindly Bent to Ease Us, Part One*. Berkeley: Dharma Publishing, 1975. The great scholar yogi of the Nyingma tradition has written here a beautifully poetical text expounding the graduated path to enlightenment.

MacKenzie, Vicki. *Reincarnation: the Boy Lama*. London: Bloomsbury, 1988. The dramatic story of the discovery of Lama Tenzin Osel Rinpoche, the Spanish child recognized as the incarnation of Lama Yeshe.

McDonald, Kathleen. *How to Meditate*. Boston: Wisdom,

1990. An excellent introduction covering the spectrum of Buddhist meditational practices, including the method for visualizing Shakyamuni Buddha.

Pabongka Rinpoche. *Liberation in the Palm of Your Hand.* Boston: Wisdom, 1991. An extensive commentary to the *Lam-rim Chen-mo* of Je Tsong Khapa. This is an authoritative yet easily readable account of the entire path to enlightenment.

——— Rabten, Geshe. *Treasury of Dharma.* London: Tharpa, 1988. This work by one of Lama Yeshe and Lama Zopa's main teachers is based on a month-long meditation course given to Westerners and is an excellent introduction to the basic practice of Tibetan Buddhism.

——— Rabten, Geshe and Geshe Ngawang Dhargyey. *Advice from a Spiritual Friend.* Boston: Wisdom, 1984. A compilation of inspiring teachings on the Mahayana tradition of thought transformation.

——— Sopa, Geshe Lhundup and Jeffrey Hopkins. *Cutting Through Appearances.* Ithaca: Snow Lion, 1989. This book unites theory and practice in one volume by including a meditation text on the graduated path with the translation for a short text on the tenets of the different Buddhist schools together with explanatory commentary.

Tarthang Tulku. *Calm and Clear.* Berkeley: Dharma, 1973. This translation of two works by the nineteenth century master Mi-pam deals with meditations on mindfulness and emptiness.

Tsong Khapa, (Tharchin, Geshe Lobsang, trans.) *The Principal Teachings of Buddhism.* Howell, NJ: Mahayana Sutra and Tantra Press, 1988. Je Tsong Khapa's teachings on the principal aspects of the Buddhist path as interpreted by Pabongka Rinpoche.

Trungpa, Chogyam. *Cutting Through Spiritual Materialism.* Boston: Shambhala, 1973. In this modern classic, a Tibetan lama with an intimate knowledge of the Western mind discusses the subtle problems facing spiritual seekers.

——Wangchen, Geshe Namgyal. *Awakening the Mind of Enlightenment*. Boston: Wisdom, 1987. A clear and simple presentation of the methods for developing inner awareness and a compassionate motivation.

Wangyal, Geshe. *The Door of Liberation*. Novato, CA: Lotsawa, 1978. A selection of important texts including the precepts of the Kadam masters and Je Tsong Khapa's *Three Principal Aspects of the Path*.

——Yeshe, Lama Thubten. *Introduction to Tantra*. Boston: Wisdom, 1987. "No other member of the tradition has ever talked about Tantra with such clarity, coherence and simplicity, and no one has summarized the essence of Tantra so well as Thubten Yeshe does here." *Religious Studies Review*.

Yeshe, Lama Thubten, et al. *Wisdom Energy 2*. Boston: Wisdom, 1979. This sequel to the present volume includes a number of talks and lectures by Lama Yeshe and several other eminent Tibetan lamas compiled in a stimulating and special collection with a very contemporary flavor.

Zopa Rinpoche, Lama Thubten. *Transforming Problems*. Boston: Wisdom, 1989. A forceful, penetrating and singularly practical teaching on through transformation in the varied experiences of everyday life.